HEALING YOUR
GRIEVING SOUL

*Companion Press is dedicated to the education and
support of both the bereaved and bereavement caregivers.
We believe that those who companion the bereaved by
walking with them as they journey in grief have a
wondrous opportunity: to help others embrace and grow
through grief—and to lead fuller, more deeply-lived lives
themselves because of this important ministry.*

Companion
P R E S S

For a complete catalog and ordering information, write or call:

Companion Press
The Center for Loss and Life Transition
3735 Broken Bow Road
Fort Collins, CO 80526
(970) 226-6050
www.centerforloss.com

HEALING YOUR GRIEVING SOUL

•

100 SPIRITUAL PRACTICES FOR MOURNERS

•

ALAN D. WOLFELT, PH.D.

Companion
P R E S S

Fort Collins, Colorado
An imprint of the Center for Loss and Life Transition

Companion Press is an imprint of the
Center for Loss and Life Transition,
3735 Broken Bow Road, Fort Collins, Colorado 80526
970-226-6050
www.centerforloss.com

Companion Press books may be purchased in bulk for sales promotions, premiums or fundraisers. Please contact the publisher at the above address for more information.

Printed in the United States of America

12 11 10 09   5 4 3 2 1

ISBN: 978-1-879651-57-9

IN GRATITUDE

A heartfelt thank you to the many colleagues, family, and friends who have provided wisdom and encouragement as I penned this book. They know who they are and that I have held them in my heart as I wrote the words that follow.

Many people contributed ideas and reflections related to this resource. Without these lovely people, I would not have had the courage to unfold this important venture. I am so very grateful to Susan Lukey, Wally Glover, Ros and Glen Crichton, and Carla and Rick Holmlund.

I have always liked the word *behold*: it means to look upon something amazing or unexpected. I'm honored that I was able to behold how people were excited to share in this attempt to help my fellow human beings nurture themselves in the spiritual realm. To each of you I say thank you so very much for your contribution of ideas that I could expand upon.

INTRODUCTION

"Spirituality often requires stillness and silence."

This book is in your hands because someone you love has died. I am so very sorry for your loss. You have been "torn apart" and have some very unique needs. Among these needs is to nurture yourself in five important areas: physically, emotionally, cognitively, socially, and spiritually. While all of these areas are vitally important, this book focuses on practical ways to nurture yourself in the spiritual realm.

When someone we love dies, it is like a deep hole implodes inside of us. It's as if the hole penetrates us and leaves us gasping for air. I have always said we mourn life losses from the inside out. In my experience it is only when we are spiritually nurtured (inside and outside) that we discover the courage to mourn openly and honestly.

I hope the spiritual practices explored in the following pages bring you some solace and help you be self-compassionate. The word compassion literally means "with passion." So, self-compassion means caring for oneself with passion. While I hope you have excellent outside support, this little book is intended to help you be kind to yourself spiritually.

I have discovered that many of us are hard on ourselves when we are in mourning. We often have inappropriate expectations of how "well" we should be doing with our grief. These expectations come from common societal messages that tell us to be strong in the face of grief. We are told to "carry on," "keep our chins up," and "keep busy." Worse yet, many of us are told, "God wouldn't give you anything more than you can bear." These and other similar messages often discourage us from practicing spiritual self-care, which, by contrast, is needed because it invites and encourages us to suspend. In actuality, when we are in grief, we need to slow down, to turn inward, to embrace our feelings of loss, and to seek and accept support. No, it is not always easy to be spiritually self-compassionate in a mourning-avoidant culture. Without doubt, spiritual self-care takes time, mindfulness, and discernment.

To integrate spiritual practices into your life demands a reminder that:

Spirituality invites you to slow down and turn inward.

Spirituality invites you to feel deeply and to believe passionately.

Spirituality invites you to get to know your authentic self.

Spirituality invites you to celebrate diversity.

Spirituality invites you to be open to the mystery.

To practice spiritual self-care doesn't mean you are feeling sorry for yourself; rather, it means you are allowing yourself to have the courage to pay attention to your "special needs." For it is in spiritually nurturing ourselves, in allowing ourselves the time and loving attention we need to journey through our grief, that we find meaning in our continued living. It is in having the courage to care for our own needs that we discover a fullness to living and loving again. That is why, if I could, I would encourage all of us when we are in the midst of grief to put down "nurture my spirit" first on our daily to-do lists.

The Mosaic World We Live In

Perhaps you have noticed that our world has gotten much smaller religiously in the last fifty years. Eastern religions and spiritual practices arrived in the United States and Canada little more than 150 years ago. Then, in the 1960s, we saw books, lectures, and workshops from folks like Thich Nhat Hanh and Ram Dass, who invited us Westerners to explore Eastern spiritual practices. This influx of Eastern traditions and practices breathed new life into spirituality in North America. Since then, on the mosaic planet we live on, there has been some (obviously, we still have a long way to go) increased understanding among faith groups concerning our differences and our similarities. While our differences still define us, our potential to borrow meaningful spiritual practices from each other unites us. The great equalizer—death—invites us to be enriched by learning from each other.

Yes, we now have the opportunity to learn from other spiritual/religious traditions other than the one we may call our own. We are witnessing an increased interest in learning from a variety of sources, and many, certainly not all, religious traditions are less circumspect and more open to a wide variety of potential sources for the discovery of meaningful spiritual practices.

In many communities today across North America, neighbors, families, friends, and coworkers uphold different religious traditions and spiritual practices. Methodists marry Jews, Catholics marry Buddhists, Baptists marry Lutherans, and we live and work side by side. Religiously and spiritually, we see attempts to communicate more and more with each other, learn together, grow together, and while we have a long way to go, this is something to celebrate and feel blessed by.

As you explore these pages that I hope and pray encourage you to nurture yourself spiritually, I recognize that spirituality and religiosity are not synonymous. In some people's lives they overlap completely; their religious lives *are* their spiritual lives. Other people have a rich spiritual lives with few or no ties to an organized religion. Obviously, each of us needs to define our own spirituality in the depths of our own hearts and minds. The paths we choose will be our own, discovered through self-examination, reflection, and spiritual transformation. What I hope this resource can do for you is offer up an opportunity to consider spiritual practices through a wide-angle lens that will support you on your grief journey.

My Personal Journey and the "Switch"

When grief and loss have touched my life, I have discovered that my own personal source of spirituality anchors me, allowing me to put my life into perspective. For me, spirituality involves a sense of connection to all things in nature, God, and the world at large. I recognize that, for some, contemplating a spiritual life in the midst of the pain of grief can be difficult.

A wise person once observed, "Spirituality is like a switch. Everybody has one; it's just that not everyone has it turned on." Sometimes, experiences of grief and loss can turn off your switch. We are human, and sometimes our switches feel stuck, or worse yet, nonexistent. Our "divine spark"—"that which gives life meaning and purpose"—feels like it has been muted. In large part, my hope is that this book helps your "spirituality switch" stay on, even if part of you wants to keep it in the off position.

Yes, life is a miracle, and we need to remind ourselves of that, during both happy and sad times. When it comes to our spiritual lives, we have an abundance of choices, all of which can be doors leading to the soul. Spirituality can be found in simple things: a sunrise or sunset; the unexpected kindness of a stranger; the rustle of the wind in the trees.

My switch is turned on when I live from a desire to see a loving God in the everyday. In the midst of grief, I can still befriend hope, and the most ordinary moment can feed my soul. Spirituality is anchored in faith, which is expecting goodness even in the worst of times. It is not about fear, which is expecting the worst even in the best of times. Spirituality reminds you that you can and will integrate losses into your life, that there is goodness in others, and that there are many pathways to Heaven.

The Openness of a Child

If you have doubts about your capacity to connect with God and the world around you, try to approach the world with the openness of a child. Embrace the pleasure that comes from the simple sights, smells, and sounds that greet your senses. You can and will find yourself rediscovering the essentials within your soul and the spirit of the world around you.

Yes, you may, in part, find yourself with this book because you have a broken heart that needs to be ministered to from both inside and out. I truly believe that acknowledging your heart is broken is the beginning of your healing. As you experience the pain of your loss—gently opening, acknowledging and allowing the suffering it has wrought diminishes but never completely vanishes. In fact, the resistance to the pain can potentially be more painful than the pain itself. Running from the pain of loss closes down our hearts and spirits. As difficult as it is, we must relinquish ourselves to the pain of grief. As Helen Keller said, "The only way to the other side is through."

Yet, going through the pain of loss is not in and of itself the goal in our grief journey. Instead, it is rediscovering life in ways that give us reason to get our feet out of bed and to make life matter. I'm certain you realize that the death of someone precious to you is not something you will ever "overcome" or "let go of." The death of someone we have given love to and received love from doesn't call out to be "resolved" or "explained," but to be experienced.

Experience is the "enforced learning of life." If anyone inappropriately tells you that "you will grow from this," remember the word ENFORCED. This is not growth you would choose. Actually, you would choose to have that special person you love back in your arms!

How to Make Use of This Book

As promised, this book contains 100 spiritual practices to help you care for yourself in mourning. Of course, spirituality is different for each of us. So, if you come to an idea that doesn't fit you, ignore it and flip to another page. However, you may want to stay open to trying some new spiritual practices and see what happens.

You'll also notice that each of the 100 ideas offer a "carpe diem," which means "seize the day." My hope is that you not relegate this book to your shelves but instead keep it handy on your nightstand or coffee table. Pick it up often and turn to any page; the carpe diem might help you seize the day by giving you a spiritual practice, action, or thought to consider today, right now, right this minute.

On a personal note, a key for me has been discovering the spiritual practices that seem to resonate with me. I grew up in a traditional faith community; I watched and learned from a variety of people whose "switches" appeared to be in the ON position. I have come to appreciate what some might term more "traditional" practices as well as some "non-traditional" practices. I have observed the simple yet lovely ways different people connect with the Divine. I have tried to integrate into my daily life those practices that seem to really connect for me.

For example, one that has really had meaning for me even when faced with grief and loss is keeping a daily gratitude journal (see Idea 94). At night before I go to bed, I write down what I have gratitude for, and that practice allows me to see some light even in the midst of the dark and find blessings in each day.

As you explore the practices in search of those that might be helpful to you in your grief journey, ask yourself: what broadens my perspective and deepens my faith? What brings me some peace and calms my fears? What deepens my connection to other people, to God, to the world, and to my essential self?

I truly believe it is essential to be supportive and non-judgmental of ourselves and others as each of us journeys to find the holy or sacred in life. I thank you for having the courage to explore the following spiritual practices and borrow the ideas that help you keep your switch in the ON position.

Alan D. Wolfelt

1.

NURTURE YOUR SPIRIT

- Nurturing your spirit relates to caring for that part of yourself that is transcendent. Your spirit speaks to you with inner messages and invites you to surround yourself with positive regard.

- You can care for your spirit in ways ranging from inspirational reading to listening to or playing music, being with those you feel support from, walking in the woods, strolling on the beach, or spending time in the company of wise people of any spiritual path.

- Nurturing your spirit means giving attention to your underlying beliefs and values. It also means being non-judgmental as you observe and appreciate people who have a different faith or spiritual outlook than you do. You can expand your own spiritual journey by going beyond your comfort zone and trying one of the practices in this book that you would not normally participate in.

CARPE DIEM

Look over the spiritual practices in this book and select one to participate in that you might not naturally be drawn toward. Try it out and be open to how it expands your capacity to nurture your spirit.

2.

EXPRESS YOUR SPIRITUALITY

- Above all, mourning is a spiritual journey of the heart and soul. Grief and loss invite you to consider why people live, why people die, and what gives life meaning and purpose. These are the most spiritual questions we have language to form.

- You can discover spiritual understanding in many ways and through many practices—prayer, worship, and meditation among them. You can nurture your spirituality in many places—nature, church, temple, mosque, monastery, retreat center, kitchen table among them. No one can "give" you spirituality from the outside in. Even when you gain spiritual understanding from a specific faith tradition, the understanding is yours alone, discovered through self-examination, reflection and spiritual transformation.

- Mourning invites you down a spiritual path at once similar to that of others yet simultaneously your own. The reality that you have picked up this book shows that you are seeking to deepen your life with the Divine Mystery. Sometimes this happens within a faith tradition through its scriptures, community of believers and teachers. Other times a book is just what you need to support and gently guide you in ways that bring comfort and hope.

CARPE DIEM

If you attend a place of worship, visit it today, either for services or an informal time of prayer and solitude. If you don't have a place of worship, perhaps you have a friend who seems spiritually grounded. Ask her how she learned to nurture her spirituality. Sometimes, someone else's ideas and practices provide just what you need to stimulate your own spiritual self-care.

3.

SET ASIDE TIME EACH DAY
FOR SPIRITUAL PRACTICE

- You get up every morning. You brush your teeth. You shower. You eat breakfast. Perhaps you read the newspaper or check your e-mail. You say hello to your family or coworkers or neighbors.

- Every day you engage in rituals of self-care. You take care of your body. You take care of your brain. You probably take care of your social self, at least to some degree. But how do you make sure you are caring for your emotional self and your spiritual self each and every day?

- Your spirit needs feeding just as much as your body does. Set aside time to feed it each day.

- What will you do with your spiritual time? You decide! Perhaps you have a favorite spiritual practice, such as yoga or meditation. Maybe you could use your daily time to try different ideas in this book.

CARPE DIEM

You know that you're supposed to exercise your body for 30 minutes a day. Start exercising your spirit for 30 minutes a day, too. Begin today.

4.

SEEK OUT A SPIRITUAL ADVISOR

- Many of us flounder in our spirituality, especially in the early weeks and months after the death of someone loved.

- Grief brings about a normal and necessary search for meaning. Why are we here? Why do the people we love have to die? What is the purpose of life? These are the most spiritually profound questions we have language to form.

- To assist you in your search for meaning and to provide you with spiritual mentoring, seek out the help of someone whom you find to be spiritually advanced or grounded.

- This person might be a member of the clergy or someone with formal religious or spiritual training, but it also might be someone who simply seems to connect well with the spiritual realm.

CARPE DIEM

Right now, make a list of three local people you look up to spiritually. Try to identify someone with whom you can meet in person periodically. Call him or her today and extend an invitation to meet for coffee.

5.

REACH OUT TO OTHERS FOR HELP

- Perhaps the most compassionate thing you can do for yourself at this difficult time is to reach out for help from others.

- Think of it this way: Grieving may be the hardest work you have ever done. And hard work is less burdensome when others lend a hand. Life's greatest challenges—getting through school, raising children, pursuing a career—are in many ways team efforts. So it should be with mourning.

- Sharing your pain with others won't make it disappear, but it will, over time, make it more bearable.

- Reaching out for help also connects you to other people and strengthens the bonds of love that make life seem worth living again. But just like gardens, good friends must be cultivated. True friends are blessings during overwhelming times such as this. If you have some, give thanks!

- When Bill Cosby's son Ennis was murdered, Mr. Cosby reached out to other families who were that day also confronted with the murder of their children. He was not alone and you aren't either.

CARPE DIEM

Call a close friend who may have distanced himself from
you since the death and tell him how much you need
him right now. Suggest specific ways he can help.

6.

TAKE GOOD CARE OF YOURSELF

- Good self-care is nurturing and necessary for mourners, yet it's something many of us completely overlook.

- Try very hard to eat well and get adequate rest. Lay your body down 2-3 times a day for 20-30 minutes, even if you don't sleep. I know—you probably don't care very much about eating well right now, and you may be sleeping poorly. But taking care of yourself is truly one way to fuel healing and to begin to embrace life again.

- Listen to what your body tells you. "Get some rest," it says. "But I don't have time," you reply. "I have things to do." "OK, then, I'll get sick so you HAVE to rest," your body says. And it *will* get sick if that's what it takes to get its needs met!

- Drink at least 5-6 glasses of water each day. Dehydration can compound feelings of fatigue and disorientation.

- Exercise not only provides you with more energy, it can give you focused thinking time. Take a 20-minute walk every day. Or, if that seems too much, a 5-minute walk. But don't over-exercise, because your body needs extra rest, as well.

- Now more than ever, you need to allow time for you.

CARPE DIEM

Are you taking a multi-vitamin? If not, now is probably a good time to start. In part, you can think of it as a spiritual self-care vitamin!

7.

BE PATIENT

- I'm sure you've realized by now that healing in grief does not usually happen quickly. And because your grief is never truly "over," you are on a lifelong journey.

- In our hurry-up North American culture, patience can be especially hard to come by. We have all been conditioned to believe that if we want something, we should be able to get it instantly.

- Yet your grief will not heed anyone's timetable—even your own. Be patient with yourself. Be patient with those around you. You are doing the best you can, as are they.

- Practicing patience means relinquishing control. Just as you cannot truly control your life, you cannot control your grief. Yes, you can set your intention to embrace your grief and take steps to mourn well, and these practices will certainly serve you well on your journey, but you cannot control the particulars of what life will continue to lay before you.

CARPE DIEM

When you are feeling impatient, silently repeat this phrase: "Let nothing disturb thee; Let nothing dismay thee; All things pass; God never changes. Patience attains all that it strives for. He who has God finds he lacks nothing: God alone suffices."— St. Teresa of Avila

8.

KNOW THAT YOU ARE LOVED

- As Jane Howard wisely observed, "Call it a clan, call it a network, call it a tribe, call it a family. Whatever you call it, whoever you are, you need one." Yes, love from family, friends, and community gives life meaning and purpose. Look around for expressions of care and concern. These are people who love you and want to be an important part of your support system.

- Some of those who love you may not know how to reach out to you, but they still love you. Reflect on the people who care about you and the ways in which your life matters.

- In contrast, if you lose this connection, you suffer alone and in isolation. You feel disconnected from the world around you. Feeling pessimistic, you may retreat even more. You begin to sever your relationships and make your world smaller. Over-isolation anchors your loss and sadness in place.

- It is vital to create a sense of community that is spiritually nurturing and responsive to the needs surrounding loss in your life. Your relationships with family, friends, and community are connected like a circle, with no end and no beginning. When you allow yourself to be a part of that circle, you find your place. You realize you belong and are a vital part of a bigger whole.

CARPE DIEM

Get out some notes and cards you have received from people who care about you. Re-read them and remind yourself that you are loved. Then, call someone you love and express gratitude that she or he is in your life.

9.

UNDERSTAND THE SIX NEEDS OF MOURNING

Need 1: Acknowledge the reality of the death

- Someone you love has died. This is probably the most difficult reality in the world to accept. Yet gently, slowly and patiently you must embrace this reality, bit by bit, day by day.

- Whether the death was sudden or anticipated, acknowledging the full reality of the loss may occur over weeks, months, even years.

- You will first acknowledge the reality of the loss with your head. Only over time will you come to acknowledge it with your heart and soul.

- At times you may push away the reality of the death. This is normal and necessary for your survival. You will come to integrate the reality in doses as you are ready.

CARPE DIEM

Tell someone about the person who died today. Talking about both the life and the death will help you work on this important need.

10.

UNDERSTAND THE SIX NEEDS OF MOURNING

Need 2: Embrace the pain of the loss

• This need requires mourners to embrace the pain of their loss—
something we naturally don't want to do. It is easier to avoid, repress,
or push away the pain of grief than it is to confront it.

• It is in embracing your grief, however, that you will learn to reconcile
yourself to it.

• In the early days after the death, your pain may seem ever-present.
Your every thought and feeling, every moment of every day, may seem
painful. During this time, you will probably need to seek refuge from
your pain. Go for a walk, read a book, watch TV, talk to supportive
friends and family about the normal things of everyday life.

• While you do need to embrace the pain of your loss, you must do it in
doses, over time. You simply cannot take in the enormity of your loss
all at once. It's healthy to seek distractions and allow yourself bits of
pleasure each day.

CARPE DIEM

If you feel up to it, allow yourself a time for embracing
pain today. Dedicate 15 minutes to thinking about and
feeling the loss. Reach out to someone who doesn't try to
take your pain away and spend some time with him.

11.

UNDERSTAND THE SIX NEEDS OF MOURNING

Need 3: Remember the person who died

- When someone loved dies, they live on in us through memory.

- To heal, you need to actively remember the person who died and commemorate the life that was lived.

- Never let anyone take your memories away in a misguided attempt to save you from pain. It's good for you to continue to display photos of the person who died. It's good to talk about memories, both happy and sad. It's good to cherish clothing and other items that belonged to her.

- In the early weeks and months of your grief, you may fear that you will forget the person who died—the details of her face, the tone of his voice, the special lilt in her walk. Rest assured that while time may blur some of your memories, as you slowly shift your relationship from one of presence to one of memory, you will indeed remember.

- Remembering the past makes hoping for the future possible.

CARPE DIEM

You might find it helpful to begin to write down memories of the person who died. This is both a healing exercise and a way to hold onto special memories forever. Today, write down at least one memory.

12.

UNDERSTAND THE SIX
NEEDS OF MOURNING

Need 4: Develop a new self-identity

• A big part of your self-identity may have been formed by the relationship you had with the person who died.

• What was your relationship? If your mother died, you may find yourself feeling orphaned. If your spouse died, you may be struggling with newfound and confusing feelings about being a widow.

• While you must work through this difficult need yourself, I can assure you that you are and always will be a child of your parent, a husband to your wife, a best friend, etc. While death may change the language that others now use about your relationship, the bonds of the relationship do not simply disintegrate and vanish. They were, they are, and they always will be.

• Still, in other ways, how you define yourself and the way society defines you is changed. You need to re-anchor yourself, to reconstruct your self-identity. This can be arduous and painful work.

CARPE DIEM

Write out a response to this prompt: I used to be _____.
Now that _____ died, I am _____. This makes me
feel _____. Keep writing as long as you want.

13.

UNDERSTAND THE SIX
NEEDS OF MOURNING

Need 5: Search for meaning

- When someone loved dies, we naturally question the meaning and purpose of life and death. Why did this person have to die? Why are we here?

- "Why?" questions may surface uncontrollably and often precede "How" questions. "Why did this happen?" comes before "How will I go on living?"

- You will almost certainly question your philosophy of life and explore religious and spiritual values as you work on this need.

- Remember that having faith or spirituality does not negate your need to mourn. If you believe in an afterlife of some kind, both you and the person who died have still lost precious time together on Earth. It's normal to feel dumbfounded and have an instinct to explore spiritual questions.

- Ultimately, you may decide that there is no answer to the question "Why did this happen?" The death may never make sense to you.

CARPE DIEM

Write down a list of "why" questions that have surfaced for you since the death. Find a friend or spiritual comforter who will explore these questions with you without thinking she has to give you answers.

14.

UNDERSTAND THE SIX NEEDS OF MOURNING

Need 6: Receive ongoing support from others

- As mourners, we need the love and understanding of others if we are to heal.

- Don't feel ashamed by your heightened dependence on others right now. If the death was recent, you may feel the need to be around people all the time. You may need to talk about the death often. You may need help getting meals together, doing laundry, completing paperwork. Don't feel bad about this. Instead, take comfort in the knowledge that others care about you.

- Unfortunately, our society places too much value on "carrying on" and "doing well" after a death. So, many mourners are abandoned by their friends and family soon after the death. Keep in mind the rule of thirds: one-third of your friends will be supportive of your need to mourn, one-third will make you feel worse, and one-third will neither help nor hinder.

- Grief is experienced in "doses" over years, not quickly and efficiently, and you will need the continued support of your friends and family for weeks, months and years.

CARPE DIEM

Sometimes your friends want to support you but don't know how. Ask. Call your closest friend right now and tell him you need his help through the coming weeks and months. Even if the death was years ago, renewing the subject with a close friend will help him understand that your grief is still very much a part of your life.

15.

LOVE YOURSELF

- Someone once astutely observed, "Love is the highest, purest, most precious of all spiritual things." Sometimes it is easier to express love to others than it is to ourselves. Yet, by feeling your own love in a more direct way, you can be transformed and open yourself to new spiritual understanding.

- Loving yourself starts with accepting yourself. If you, as a living, unique human being, are unable to value who you are, who can? If part of your need to mourn is anchored in recapturing your capacity to give love out, you must start by giving love in. Honoring *you* is part of your need right now and nobody else can do it from the inside out.

- Loving yourself means recognizing you, seeing you, and honoring you. In part, it is about celebrating yourself. It is a privilege to be yourself. You have been given the opportunity to feel, to see, to live life with both its challenges and opportunities. Sometimes, in the midst of the pain of your grief, you can forget this. You may feel alone, questioning your existence, not liking who you are, and being self-disparaging. Yet, even in the face of loss, remember: It is a gift to be alive, and just being born into the world is a compliment. Being able to give and receive love and then mourn your life losses is part of the beauty of being alive. If you forget to affirm the truth that "blessed are those that mourn," you insult the consciousness that gave you life.

CARPE DIEM

Dedicate this day to loving yourself. Find a quiet place to sit in stillness. Now, remind yourself of your inner beauty and unique self. Befriend your emotional and spiritual strengths, your humor, your intelligence, your sensitivity, your wisdom, your gifts. From this conscious, loving acceptance, your capacity to eventually open yourself to loving life again can come forth. Yes, love yourself!

16.

PRAY

- Prayer is mourning because prayer means taking your feelings and articulating them to someone else. Even when you pray silently, you're forming words for your thoughts and feelings and you're offering up those words to a presence outside yourself.

- Someone wise once noted, "Our faith is capable of reaching the realm of mystery."

- Did you know that real medical studies have shown that prayer can actually help people heal?

- If you believe in a higher power, pray. Pray for the person who died. Pray for your questions about life and death to be answered. Pray for the strength to embrace your pain and to go on to find continued meaning in life and living. Pray for others affected by this death.

- Many places of worship have prayer lists. Call yours and ask that your name be added to the prayer list. On worship days, the whole congregation will pray for you. Often many individuals will pray at home for those on the prayer list, as well.

CARPE DIEM

Bow your head right now and say a silent prayer. If you are out of practice, don't worry; just let your thoughts flow naturally.

17.

CRY

- Tears are a natural cleansing and healing mechanism. They rid your body of stress chemicals. It's OK to cry. In fact, it's good to cry when you feel like it. What's more, tears are a form of mourning. They are sacred!

- Your pain, your grief, your overwhelming loss disturbs the world around you. Disturb the quiet with your soul's cry.

- On the other hand, don't feel bad if you aren't crying a lot. Not everyone is a crier.

- You may find that those around you are uncomfortable with your tears. As a society, we're often not so good at witnessing others in pain. Don't let those people take your grief away from you.

- Explain to your friends and family that you need to cry right now and that they can help by allowing you to.

- You may even find yourself *keening*, which means a loud wailing or wordless crying out in lament for the dead. Keening is an instinctive form of mourning. It gives voice to your soul's profound pain at a time when words are inadequate.

- You may find yourself crying at unexpected times or places. If you need to, excuse yourself and retreat to somewhere private. Or better yet, go ahead and cry openly and honestly, unashamed of your tears of overwhelming grief.

CARPE DIEM

If you feel like it, have a good cry today. Find a safe place to embrace your pain and cry as long and as hard as you want to.

18.

SCHEDULE SOMETHING THAT GIVES YOU PLEASURE EACH AND EVERY DAY

- When we're in mourning, often we need something to look forward to, a reason to get out of bed today.

- It's hard to look forward to each day when you know you will be experiencing pain and sadness.

- To counterbalance your normal and necessary mourning, plan something you enjoy doing every day.

- Reading, baking, going for a walk, having lunch with a friend, playing computer games—whatever brings you enjoyment. (Just remember—no inappropriate risk-taking.)

CARPE DIEM

What's on tap for today? Squeeze in something you enjoy, no matter how hectic your schedule.

19.

BREATHE AND MEDITATE

- Deep breathing and meditation can change your life. They are also spiritual practices you can do anytime and anyplace. The benefits are physical, emotional, and spiritual. Meditation invites your body into a more relaxed physical state, causes more restful sleep, lowers your blood pressure, increases oxygen circulation, improves your immune system, increases your ability to concentrate, calms your mind, and stimulates an overall feeling of well-being.

- Give yourself five full minutes to concentrate on your breathing. Imagine that you're inhaling the spiritual energy you need to help you integrate loss into your life and that you're exhaling your feelings of sadness and grief. No, this doesn't make your grief go away, but it helps soothe your soul.

- Breathing opens you up. Grief may have naturally closed you down. The power of breath helps to fill your empty spaces. The old wisdom of "count to ten" is all about taking a breath to open up space for something to happen. The paradox is that in slowing down, you create divine momentum that invites you to continue to mourn.

- There are many resources available to help you learn how to meditate. One of my personal favorites is a classic simply titled *How to Meditate*, by Lawrence LeShan (Bantam Books, available in paperback).

- A well-known writer on Christian spiritual disciplines, Richard Foster, believes that Christian meditation focuses not on the emptying of the mind, but rather on the filling up of the mind with God.

CARPE DIEM

Make a commitment right now to learn how to meditate. Pick up the book noted above within the next three days. Just a few minutes of meditation each day will provide you a wonderful spiritual perspective on where you are in your life's journey.

20.

KEEP A JOURNAL

- Journals can be a gentle, self-compassionate way to nurture your emotions of grief and loss. The process of writing down what you are experiencing invites you to pause and be conscious of what you are thinking and feeling. Journaling gives you that time and honors the need for you to take your inner thoughts and feelings of grief (your internal response to loss) and convert them to mourning (the shared social response to loss). Without doubt you have heard the wise words, "Blessed are those who mourn." So, journaling helps support your need to mourn openly and honestly.

- Journaling is private and independent, yet it's still expressing your grief outside of yourself. The process of putting the written word on paper is profoundly helpful because it:

  - creates a safe place of solace, a place where you can fully express yourself no matter what you are experiencing.
  - clears out your naturally overwhelmed mind and full heart.
  - creates an opportunity to balance your life between the sad and the happy.
  - strengthens your awareness of how your grief journey changes over time.
  - maps out your transformation as you journey through grief.

- As Annie Dillard observed, "When you write, you lay out a line of words. The line of words is a miner's pick, a woodcarver's gouge, a surgeon's probe. You wield it, and it digs a path you follow." To this I would add that a line of words can be a lifeline when you are in the midst of grief and loss.

CARPE DIEM

Stop by your local bookstore and chose a notebook you like the look and feel of. Set aside some time this evening and spend a few minutes writing your first entry.

21.

ALLOW GOD TO SPEAK TO YOU

- We hear so much about praying to God, but what about allowing God to speak to you?

- In the Bible, the book of Exodus chronicles the story of God delivering his people, the Israelites, from the bondage of slavery. Those of you who have not read the book of Exodus may be familiar with the epic film *The Ten Commandments*, in which a young Charlton Heston plays the role of Moses.

- Exodus Chapter 3 picks up the story with a young shepherd named Moses tending a flock of sheep. While tending the flock, Moses came across a strange sight. He had encountered a bush that was on fire but did not burn up. His curiosity got the best of him, and so he wandered over to get a closer look. It was there that Moses encountered the presence of God, and it was there that Moses heard God's plan for a suffering nation.

- Our mourning experiences touch us in profound ways at the very core of our body, mind, and soul. Lamenting can be a result of intense suffering; it is our way of communicating with God.

- But Moses also shows us that God communicates with us. You may not find God in a burning bush, but you may find Him in the stillness of the moment, in the wind, in the natural world that surrounds us. Yes, God speaks to us if we take the time to listen.

CARPE DIEM

Seek out those quiet, still places and listen to God's voice. Open yourself to the verse "Be still and know that I am God." And remember that one of the final things God said to Moses was "I will be with you."

22.

JUST BE

- You may have heard it said that there is no past, there is no future, there is only this moment.

- In *The Power of Now*, Eckhart Tollé encourages us to truly be present in the current moment. "Life is now," he writes. "There was never a time when your life was not now, nor will there ever be Nothing ever happened in the past; it happened in the Now. Nothing will ever happen in the future; it will happen in the Now."

- The challenge is that it is really *hard* to live in the moment. Our minds constantly revisit the past and think forward to the future. Our egos dwell on what was and what will be.

- Tollé and others believe that your mind is different from your spirit. Your mind is the house of the ego; your soul is the house of the spirit. Your spirit—your essence—can observe the egoic antics of the mind. Your ego is earthbound; your spirit is timeless.

- The next time your mind takes you away from the present and into worry and fear, allow your spirit to watch your mind and smile at its earthly obsessions.

CARPE DIEM

Attend to the now. Drop everything and just be for
five minutes. When your monkey mind starts to
chatter, silence it by repeating the mantra *om*.

23.

CREATE

- Get in touch with the Creator by creating. Make something that expresses your feelings or honors the loss you are mourning.

- Is there a creative activity that you find you lose yourself in—that you get so involved in that you lose all track of time and place and you become immersed in your creative process? If so, that's the kind of activity you want to do now.

- Write. Paint. Sew. Scrapbook. Knit. Garden. Cook. Play an instrument. Decorate. Organize. All of these activities are forms of creation. Pick one that moves you.

CARPE DIEM

Make something today.

24.

SIGH

- Sighing is an expression of letting go. When we sigh, we resign ourselves to something. We accept something, though perhaps it is something we didn't want to accept.

- In Romans 8 it says that when there are no words for our prayer, the spirits intervene and pray for us in sighs deeper than anything that can be expressed in words.

- Sigh deeply. Sigh whenever you feel like it. With each sigh, you are acknowledging that you are not in total control of your life. You are accepting what is.

- Each sigh is your prayer.

CARPE DIEM

Right now, take a deep breath and sigh. Do this
ten times in a row. How do you feel?

25.

ALLOW YOURSELF TO RECEIVE

• Many of us are better at giving than receiving. Yet, there is a reciprocal relationship between the two. In order to receive, we must give. And in order to give, we must receive.

• Select a supportive friend to assist you with the following. Sit across from your friend. Be silent for two to three minutes, then have your friend tell you something he admires or appreciates about you. Be receptive.

• Take in what your friend shares with an open heart. Notice where you are uncomfortable or find yourself wanting to discount what your friend says.

• Breathe deeply for a minute as you continue to open yourself to this gift of receiving. Sit with it until you can fully accept this verbal gift. Show your gratitude by nonverbally saying thank you.

CARPE DIEM

Carry out the same process outlined above for your friend. Then repeat the process, going to a deeper level of truth. Observe how your connection and bond with your friend increases. As you learn to receive and give, the separation between giver and receiver disappears.

26.

FIND THE BARNABASES IN YOUR LIFE

- One of the significant contributors in the development of the early Christian church was a man named Joseph of Cypress (Acts 4, Verse 36). Joseph's nickname was Barnabas, meaning "son of encouragement." Barnabas was one of those individuals who believed in people when others wouldn't. He always thought the best of people, was generous with his time, and was always ready to lend a hand.

- When his good friend and coworker wanted to give up on a young man named John Mark, because he had left them and returned home when things got tough, Barnabas gave John Mark a second chance. Even against the advice of others, Barnabas hung in for John Mark when others wouldn't.

- Barnabas understood that what John Mark needed at that very moment was encouragement, not judgment; understanding, not advice; compassion, not criticism; acknowledgment, not minimization; and companionship, not treatment. Barnabas never shamed anyone for what they had done or how they felt, but instead gave to all those he encountered the gift of encouragement. People were free to be authentic in the presence of Barnabas.

CARPE DIEM

Make a list of the Barnabases in your life, and then reach out and spend some time with them. Allow their gift of encouragement to support you in your journey through grief. In other words, bask in the spiritual companionship of an encourager.

27.

CENTER YOURSELF

- Centering yourself is about letting go of resistance and going with the movement below your feet. When you are centered you don't let things that really don't matter in the big picture of life bother you. Therefore, it doesn't really matter what the weather is like outside, what table you get at a restaurant, if the stock market goes up or down, if the traffic is slow, etc. When you are centered, you are not affected by externals.

- If you are externally focused, you let little things "get to you" in ways they shouldn't. You get out of balance and are not centered internally —body, mind and spirit. Out of balance, you will likely feel empty and lost...always looking for something "outside of yourself" to fill you up. Yet, nothing out there can.

- When you are centered, you are more aware of the environment in and around you. You have more clarity and focus, and your intuition is refined. Your fear diminishes markedly and you know you can make it through the wilderness of your grief.

CARPE DIEM

Nurture friendships with hope-filled, centered people rather than "negative" or "cynical" people. People who are complainers are not centered, and are letting the world around them affect their capacity for joy...and yours if you allow it. When you use discernment to spend time with "centered" friends, you are creating a more stable environment for yourself.

28.

CONSIDER YOURSELF IN "SPIRITUAL INTENSIVE CARE"

- Something painful has happened in your life. Something assaulting to the very core of your being.

- Your spirit has been deeply injured. Just as your body cannot be expected to recover immediately from a brutal attack, neither can your psyche.

- Imagine that you've suffered a severe physical injury and are in your hospital's intensive care unit. Your friends and family surround you with their presence and love. The medical staff attends to you constantly. Your body rests and recovers.

- This is the kind of care you need and deserve right now. The blow you have suffered is no less devastating than this imagined physical injury. Allow others to take care of you. Ask for their help. Give yourself as much resting time as possible. Take time off work. Let household chores slide. Especially in the early weeks and months after a death, don't expect—indeed, don't try—to carry on with your normal routine.

CARPE DIEM

Close your eyes and imagine yourself in "spiritual intensive care." Where are you? What kind of care are you receiving? From whom? Arrange a weekend or a week of the spiritual intensive care you most need.

29.

MARK IMPORTANT DATES ON YOUR CALENDAR

- Birthdays, anniversaries and other special days are important because they present opportunities to acknowledge and spend time with people you care about.

- After someone loved has died, these same dates are important spiritual dates of connection. Yes, these special days can be painful, but the pain means that you are embracing your feelings. This is a normal and necessary part of grief.

- When birthdays come round for people you love who are still alive, instead of giving them a tangible gift, write them a special note of love and gratitude. They will cherish these notes for the rest of their lives.

CARPE DIEM

Take your calendar off the wall and spend a few minutes jotting down the birthdays, anniversaries and death dates of all your beloved friends and family members. When a special date comes up, take a few minutes to acknowledge the person or the relationship heralded by the date.

30.

SOW SEEDS OF HOPE

- A time-honored and healthy spiritual tradition of self-nurturing can be found in working with the earth. Gardening can bring you a sense of satisfaction and a feeling of oneness with nature.

- If the thought of formal gardening overwhelms you, simply try a seed garden. Look through a seed catalog for some little miracles. Easy-to-grow seed choices include: bush-type sweet peas, morning glories, impatiens, nasturtiums, cosmos, forget-me-nots, and all kinds of sunflowers. Fill small pots (clay or plastic) with seed-starting soil. Moisten with water and then sprinkle your seeds over the surface, pressing lightly with your fingertips. Place your pots in a sheltered location. You will now experience daily solace as you care for your seed babies. Water every other day or so and be ready to transplant to a larger pot when they are around three inches tall.

- Through nature and various forms of gardening, you will witness the miracle of life and find renewal and meaning in your own.

CARPE DIEM

Research the gardens or parks open to the public in your area.
Go for a visit. Also, watch the papers for gardening shows
and garden tours. Bask in the renewal of your spirit!

31.

BE GENEROUS WITH YOUR TIME AND CONCERN

- Generosity is giving from your heart and sharing the essence of yourself. Generosity is being in sync with the greater good. It is helping others in such a way that "mine" and "yours" are not part of your thinking.

- Being generous is anchored in a reciprocal relationship: You give and you get, you get and you give. When you are experiencing grief and loss, you must permit yourself to receive before you give of yourself. But, over time, and with active mourning, you may discover yourself wanting to give.

- Review your life for the ways in which you are generous. Think of the people you are close to and how you give yourself to them. Reflect on the ways you have given to others in your workplace or in your faith community. Think of the ways you have been available to friends to lift them up at a time when they were down.

- Generosity has many levels and forms of expression. You can give away possessions you no longer need but someone else can use. You can gift someone with a book you believe may help him. You can try to be as totally present to someone as you possibly can. You can unconditionally love the people around you.

CARPE DIEM

Find a place you can do some volunteer work in a way that gives expression to your generosity—at a hospice, a homeless shelter, a hospital, a humane society. As you share yourself with those in need, witness how your heart opens up and you not only give, you receive.

32.

FIND COMFORT IN THE ELEMENTS

- Ancient scientists thought the world was made up of the four elements of air, fire, earth, and water. By definition, elements are pure, basic, simple. If you try, you can find comfort and meaning in each of them.

- Air: Breathe deeply. Practice yogic breathing. Stand in the wind.

- Fire: Light a candle in your loved one's memory. Build a fire in a fireplace and sit in spiritual contemplation while you watch the flames dance.

- Earth: Garden. Plant bulbs. Start a compost pile.

- Water: Take a long bath. Go for a swim. Walk in the rain. Play in the sprinkler.

CARPE DIEM

Each of the 12 signs of the zodiac is associated with one of the four elements. Look up which element your zodiac sign represents, what the element means astrologically speaking, and contemplate whether you think it's a true fit for you.

33.

OBSERVE THE SABBATH

- The word "Sabbath" comes from the old Hebrew *shabbath*, which literally means "to rest."

- Just as God rested on the 7th day of creation, Jews and Christians "keep the Sabbath" by resting and connecting with God on Saturday or Sunday, respectively. Those who strictly keep the Sabbath do no work whatsoever on their day of rest.

- You may choose to strictly observe a religious Sabbath as a day of renewal and connection with your Maker. Or you may choose to rest and rejuvenate one day a week as a way to embrace your spirituality.

- If you observe a Sabbath day, you will be dedicating a portion of your life to your spiritual well-being. And that, regardless of your doctrine or creed, is a healthy, healing, ennobling practice.

CARPE DIEM

Observe the Sabbath this week. Create Sabbath-day rituals that safeguard this day as a sacrosanct spiritual day for you.

34.

SPEND TIME IN "THIN PLACES"

- In the Celtic tradition, "thin places" are spots where the separation between the physical world and the spiritual world seem tenuous. They are places where the veil between Heaven and earth, between the holy and the everyday, are so thin that when we are near them, we intuitively sense the timeless, boundless spiritual world.

- There is a Celtic saying that Heaven and earth are only three feet apart, but in the thin places that distance is even smaller.

- Thin places are usually outdoors, often where water and land meet or land and sky come together. You might find thin places on a riverbank, a beach, or a mountaintop.

- Go to a thin place to pray, to walk, or to simply sit in the presence of the holy.

CARPE DIEM

Your thin places are anywhere that fills you with awe and a sense of wonder. They are spots that refresh your spirit and make you feel closer to God. Go to a thin place today and sit in contemplative silence.

35.

WRITE A POEM

- Poetry is the music of language. It is sound and imagery and rhythm delivered in little packets.

- Poetry compresses great meaning into a few carefully chosen words, and as such, it can be very emotional and spiritual.

- You can write a poem if you try. It doesn't need to follow any particular rules. It doesn't need to rhyme or have a certain meter. It can be and say anything you'd like.

- An *elegy* is a poem that remembers someone who has died. Perhaps you would like to write an elegy in memory of someone you love and miss very much.

CARPE DIEM

Write a poem to God today that expresses what
you're thinking and feeling right now.

36.

SIT IN SILENCE AND SOLITUDE

- The mystery of grief invites you to honor the need for periods of silence and solitude. As you quiet yourself, you sustain an open heart and a gentle spirit. Mother Teresa often said, "The beginning of prayer is silence."

- You may not have access to a cloistered monastery, a walk in the woods, or a stroll on the beach, but you do have the capacity to quiet yourself. Consciously hush yourself and place trust in the peace you help initiate. As you sit with silence, you acknowledge that you value the need to suspend, slow down, and turn inward as part of the grief journey. Giving attention to the instinct to mourn from the inside out requires that you befriend silence and respect how vital it is to your healing journey.

- Many of the symptoms of grief are invitations to the need for silence and solitude. Disorganization, confusion, searching and yearning and the lethargy of grief try to slow you down and invite a need for you to savor silence. Yes, astutely observed, "For many afflictions, silence is the best remedy."

- Silence contains the ingredients that can bring some peace in the midst of the wilderness. The forces of grief weigh heavy on your heart. Silence serves to lift up your heart and create much-needed space to give attention to your grief.

CARPE DIEM

Today, be silent for a while—silent with yourself and with God. For many people, this is a difficult spiritual practice, but one that is well worth the effort.

37.

EXPERIENCE THE SUNRISE AND SUNSET

- The sun is a powerful symbol of life and renewal. Both sunrise and sunset are grand experiences that touch your soul. If you want to feel surrounded by God and the heavens, make use of these opportunities to bring some inner peace and solace to your day.

- When was the last time you watched a sunrise or sunset? Do you remember being touched by its beauty and power? Grief and loss remind you to appreciate the beginning and end of each day of your life. Why not allow yourself to be companioned by the rising and the setting of the sun?

- Yes, there is something so captivating about the rising and setting of the sun. The brilliant color can give your whole world a different perspective. It is a time to pause, be still, quiet your mind, and open your heart. You can appreciate and trust that out of your darkness will eventually come the light.

CARPE DIEM

Find a place that offers you a great view for either a sunrise or sunset. You may want to go alone or invite a supportive friend to come along. Embrace your personal transformation and feel blessed by the dawning of a new day or the setting of a glorious sun.

38.

GO TO EXILE

- Choosing to spend time alone is an essential self-nurturing spiritual practice. It affords you the opportunity to be unaffected by others' wants and needs.

- It is impossible to really know yourself if you never take time to withdraw from the demands of daily living. Alone time does not mean you are being selfish. Instead, you will experience rest and renewal in ways you otherwise would not. A lack of alone time produces heightened confusion and a muting of your life force.

- Getting away from it all can become your refuge. So much of modern life invites you to keep busy—e-mail, cell phones, satellite TV, all competing for your attention. Yet, when you have special mourning needs, the last thing you need is distraction. Remember, this time of exile is not only for you. As you rest and renew, you can also better meet the needs of those who depend on you. Your human spirit is naturally compassionate, and once you feel restored, your instinct to be kind and generous to those around you will be revitalized.

- Even Jesus went to exile. He modeled the simple spiritual practice of rest and alone time as a natural, nourishing, and valuable companion to times of busyness. Jesus would sometimes send people away, disappear without warning or explanation, and retreat to a place of rest. If Jesus went to exile, so can you!

- Within your exiled time and space will evolve the insights and blessings that come to the surface only in stillness and with time. Schedule alone time on a regular basis. Don't shut out your family and friends altogether, but do answer the call for contemplative solitude.

CARPE DIEM

Schedule one hour of solitude into your day today.

39.

BASK IN THE PRESENT MOMENT

- The here and now is the resting place for your heart and soul. You can consciously go to this place whenever you choose to. Here you can rest from the griefs of the past and the fears of the future.

- In the present moment comes the richness of the life that you search for. The felt experience of happiness and joy can be discovered in the present moment. To focus all of your attention in the present moment is to surrender yourself completely to whatever and whoever is with you. If you stay still you may even experience the presence of God.

- There are a variety of ways to develop the capacity to be present in the very moment. Deep breathing or meditation will not only calm your physical heart but will also help to direct your attention to your innermost feelings. Paying attention to what form of creativity naturally engages your full attention can also help you fully engage in the moment. In joyous creativity, you can enter a timeless dimension and invite tranquility into your life. Examples might include journaling, expressive arts, doing memory books. Doing something creative that you love will release worry and literally invite you to "take a breather" from other demands in your life.

CARPE DIEM

Today, engage fully in each moment of your experience. Feel the courage that grows as you embrace each moment and all that it holds.

40.

BEFRIEND EIGHT UNIVERSAL HEALING PRINCIPLES

• Eight healing principles, used in the majority of cultures, can help
sustain your physical, emotional, cognitive, social and spiritual
well-being. Explore the list below and note which of the universal
principles you are embracing and which you are neglecting.

SUPPORT HEALTH AND WELL-BEING	NON-SUPPORTIVE OF HEALTH AND WELL-BEING
Balanced diet	Unbalanced diet
Daily and weekly exercise	Lack of exercise
Time for fun, play, and laughter	Loss of humor and lack of fun and play
Music, sonics, and chanting	Lack of music, sonics, and chanting
Love, touch, and support systems	Lack of love, touch, and support systems
Engaged in interests, hobbies, and creative purpose	Lack of interests, hobbies, and creative purpose
Nature, beauty, and healing environments	Lack of nature, beauty, and healing environments
Faith and belief in the supernatural	Lack of faith and belief in the supernatural

CARPE DIEM

Make a commitment to rebalance those areas that are not
supportive to your overall well-being. Get out a piece of paper
right now and write out an "action plan for creating balance."

41.

READ FROM THE HOLY
BOOK OF YOUR CHOICE

- Whether you are a member of a formal religion or not, you may find wisdom and comfort in the world's great holy books.

- Read several verses from the Bible, the Torah, or the Koran. Reflect quietly on what you have read, then repeat the process with a few additional verses.

- Try reading passages from a holy book *not* of your religion. See if this opens up new insight and understanding for you.

- Try reading from the Tao Te Ching. This ancient Chinese text, whose title means "The Way," offers at once a very old and a very contemporary understanding of spirituality.

CARPE DIEM

Starting today, try reading a passage from a holy book each night before you turn out your light. In the dark, reflect on the words you have read and instead of assessing them analytically, allow their mystery to simply lull you to sleep.

42.

WALK A LABYRINTH

- In our lives, we are all on a path. Your life's path is now taking you through a season of grief.

- Spiritual labyrinths are now available for people to walk at many public places across the world. As you walk the labyrinth, you trust that your journey will bring you to your destination. All you need to do is walk. Even though the path may have many twists and turns, it always leads to where you need to go. There are no dead ends. There are no wrong turns. There is only walking.

- Perhaps it will help you to think of your grief as a labyrinth, not as a maze. In a maze you have to make decisions about which way to turn. You have to problem solve. If you choose poorly, you may get stuck. In a labyrinth, however, all you can do is follow the path that is laid before you. If your grief journey is a labyrinth, you can trust that if you follow the path that is laid before you, you will go deep into the center then slowly out again, emerging with a deeper understanding of your life's purpose.

- May your steps enrich your faith and your prayer life and support you in your journey through grief.

CARPE DIEM

Call around today to locate a labyrinth near your home or workplace. Take a half hour out of your day to walk the labyrinth. Before you begin, stop to center yourself. As you walk, observe the process. As you exit the labyrinth, acknowledge the ending with a transition phrase, such as *amen*.

43.

VISIT A BUTTERFLY GARDEN

- Butterflies are powerful symbols of transformation and metamorphosis. They are also a totem that can connect you to positivity, joy, and the Divine.

- Many states now have indoor butterfly gardens that are open year-round. It's quite wonderful to walk into one of these large greenhouses and be greeted by the dewy habitat and the fluttering of thousands of lovely butterfly wings.

- The North American Butterfly Association is a nonprofit whose mission is to increase public enjoyment and conservation of butterflies. They publish *American Butterflies Magazine*, a beautiful publication full of (to my way of thinking) spiritual photos of butterflies in nature. You'll receive *American Butterflies* if you become a member. To learn more, visit naba.org.

CARPE DIEM

Visit a butterfly garden—indoors or out—sometime in the next couple of days. As you watch the butterflies dance, imagine that your soul is like a butterfly...and that you, too, can have that lighter-than-air, in-the-moment feeling again.

44.

SPEND TIME WITH A PET

- Pets can be a wonderful source of comfort during times of grief. You can be needy, depressed, confused—and your pets still love you. They don't pressure you to "keep busy" or "carry on;" they don't ask you to "let go of" or "resolve" your grief. Your pets love you regardless of your weight, haircut, or body shape. Yes, your pets love you without judgment. And you feel that love and appreciate its steadfast presence in your life. Unlike many things in life, with a pet you comparatively give so little and get so much back in return.

- We pet lovers sometimes call our pets "companion animals" because they are in fact our companions. Not only can pets be your companions, but they can also help meet your need for physical contact. As you touch your pet, you are comforted, calmed, and grounded.

- Caring for and enjoying the company of animals—dogs, cats, horses, birds, deer, even fish—can offer an abundant supply of solace that many medical studies have found can help you live a longer and healthier life. Giving your attention to animals also requires you to slow down, be quiet, and become more aware of your environment. That, in turn, leads to a renewed sense of wonder and gratitude for the marvels that the world contains.

CARPE DIEM

If you have a pet, spend extra time with her today. If you don't, arrange to borrow an animal from a friend for the day.

45.

LISTEN TO THE MUSIC

- Music, perhaps more than any other external experience, has the capacity to bring you home to yourself and to restore your broken heart. Beautiful music can communicate to you on many different levels. Music can take you to your favorite place or to another world.

- Music transforms you, taking you to a "safe place" in your soul, helping you feel that you and the world around you are filled with grace and peace. Music can uplift your mood, soothe you when you are agitated, and open you to harmony, beauty, love, and generosity.

- Beautiful music that nurtures your being is by its very nature healing. It restores and relaxes you in ways beyond words. Music allows you to access spirit through sound. Music can infuse your body, mind, and spirit, and bring an inner calmness that comforts your grief-filled nerves. Music encourages you to express your grief from the inside to mourning on the outside. Music is an invitation to feel whatever you feel—sometimes even paradoxical emotions, such as happiness and sadness at once.

CARPE DIEM

Commit yourself to bring music into your daily life and
open yourself to the spiritual nurturing it brings.

46.

GO ON A PILGRIMAGE

- Pilgrimage to a sacred place is common to all religions—Christianity, Judaism, Hinduism, Islam, Native American, to name a few. The literal definition of a pilgrimage is a long journey or search, especially one of exalted purpose or moral significance.

- Grief is certainly a long search—a search for meaning, reconciliation, and peace. What search do humans undertake that has a more exalted purpose?

- Going on a pilgrimage to a sacred place is a mark of respect and often invites spiritual renewal and inner harmony to those who make the journey. From the beginning days of the Christian church, pilgrims visited the graves of the Apostles and the martyrs. The great centers of Christian medieval pilgrimage were Jerusalem, Rome, the tomb of Saint James of Compostela in Spain, and the shrine of Saint Thomas Becket in Canterbury, England.

- In your spiritual tradition, what sacred places do followers visit?

CARPE DIEM

Make plans today to go on a pilgrimage to a sacred place
that connects you to your religion or spirituality.

47.

EXPLORE YOGA

- Yoga is a three thousand year-old practice that originated from Indian spiritual teachings, a mixture of physical postures, meditation, and deep breathing. Yoga strengthens you physically, emotionally, and spiritually, and that helps you on your grief journey. Many traditions acknowledge that being on a spiritual path is like being a warrior. To practice yoga can help you be a peaceful warrior and inspire your capacity to authentically mourn.

- All yoga postures involve what are called *pranayamas*, or breathing purifications, that enhance inner tranquility. How you breathe influences the level of calm you feel. You need to breathe deeply to bring oxygen to your cells and rid the body of toxins. Yoga helps you learn to take long, slow, deep breaths that help center you and remind you to nurture your spiritual life. Yogic breathing infuses your body with *prana*, or energy.

- Because your body is unique, yoga should be individualized to best meet your needs. Yoga, which means union or wholeness, is a science and an art, based on time-tested techniques. It is probably best learned with a teacher who can coach you to learn poses and practices best suited to you. If you are new to yoga, you will want to start with a class for beginners and down the line perhaps explore other types of intermediate and advanced practices.

CARPE DIEM

Create an action plan to sign up to take an "Introduction
to Yoga" class. Pick up your phone book right now
and call to get scheduled for your first session.

48.

FORGIVE

- You may be harboring some spiteful feelings about the death of someone loved. Perhaps you are angry at a medical caregiver. Maybe you're upset at friends and family who haven't been there for you in your time of need. Maybe you are mad at the person who died.

- Forgiveness is an act of surrender. If you surrender your resentment, you are freeing yourself of a very heavy load. You are surrendering your human feelings of judgment to the only One who is truly in a position to judge. Don't go to your own grave angry.

- Forgive. Write letters of forgiveness if this will help you unburden yourself, even if you never send the letters.

- And while you're at it, don't forget to forgive yourself. Self-recrimination is negative energy. If you did something wrong, acknowledge, apologize, and forgive.

- This Idea calls to mind this poem by William Arthur Ward, an American pastor and teacher:

  Before you speak, listen.
  Before you write, think.
  Before you spend, earn.
  Before you invest, investigate.
  Before you criticize, wait.
  Before you pray, forgive.
  Before you quit, try.
  Before you retire, save.
  Before you die, give.

CARPE DIEM

Today, call or stop by to visit someone you've been holding a grudge against. Tell this person you've missed her company and would like to catch up.

49.

CARRY A TOUCHSTONE

- A touchstone is a standard of quality or excellence against which you can measure other things.

- Let's say one of your own spiritual touchstones is "seeking peace." When you are deciding how to react in a difficult situation, you might be tempted to explode in anger. But you stop to consider your "seeking peace" touchstone and instead decide that an angry outburst would be counterproductive.

- You can literally carry a stone in your pocket to remind you of your spiritual touchstones, or intentions. Whenever you're feeling your grief or struggling with a thought or feeling, put your hand in your pocket and rub your "touchstone." The stone's smooth surface and the rubbing motion will help center you and return you to your place of spiritual intention.

CARPE DIEM

Visit a rock shop today and pick out a small, polished
stone you can carry in your pocket wherever you go.

50.

KNIT OR DO NEEDLEWORK

- Many people find the repetitive motion and calm concentration of knitting and other needlework a spiritual practice.

- As you learn to knit, crochet, embroider, tat lace, do crewelwork or other needlework and become proficient at it, you see that you can at once be mindful of the handwork you are practicing and at the same time detached from the here and now. You knit and you purl, you knit and you purl, over and over and over again. The task requires sufficient concentration that your mind cannot get wholly caught up in fears and worries, yet not so much concentration that you cannot meditate or talk to others.

- Knitting and needlework are also a metaphor for your grief journey. You knit one stitch at a time just as you will live one day at a time until you die. If you proceed with care and intention, you will in the end create something meaningful—a scarf, an understanding.

- You can even find a number of books on the subject: *Zen and the Art of Knitting, Knitting into the Mystery, The Knitting Sutra, Knitting Heaven and Earth, The Knitting Way: A Guide to Spiritual Discovery.*

CARPE DIEM

Knit a prayer shawl and wear the shawl during your daily spiritual practice time. Better yet, knit two prayer shawls and give one to someone else who needs your love and support.

51.

FAST

- Since ancient times, fasting has been a way of emptying yourself out so that you can be filled with spirit.

- Spiritual leaders of all faiths and in all ages have fasted in an attempt to achieve mental and spiritual clarity. Moses, Gandhi, Jesus, Buddha, Mohammed—all fasted during their spiritual journeys.

- Fasting in the Buddhist monastic community is considered an ascetic practice, a *dhutanga* practice. *Dhutanga* means "to shake up" or "invigorate."

- Try a 24-hour or sun-up to sundown fast. Stay hydrated by drinking lots of liquids, including juices for some calories. Prepare yourself spiritually for the fast by meditating or praying your intentions for the fasting period.

- Be certain you are in good enough health to fast. If you are unsure, get a medical check-up before beginning a fast.

CARPE DIEM

Try skipping one meal today. Set your intention for this mini-fast at the beginning of the day and return your thoughts to this intention as your hunger gains your attention during the day.

52.

SCULPT

- What is the shape of your loss? Try working with clay, modeling clay, or playdough to find out.

- Dig your fingers into the clay and allow them to shape the material into something that feels right. It doesn't have to be representative of a real person, place, or thing—but it might be.

- Remember, you aren't creating a masterpiece—you're simply living in the moment and making what your soul is guiding you to make, right here, right now.

- When you're done with your sculpture, sit with it for a while and notice its shape and lines, its colors and textures. What does your sculpture say on behalf of your spirit today?

CARPE DIEM

Stop by an art supply store and buy some soft sculpture materials today.

53.

TEND YOUR GARDEN

- Many people who love to garden find it to be a deeply spiritual experience. They find peace in the garden, in part because they commune with the earth and in part because of the visual beauty of their plants and flowers.

- Working in the garden and giving birth to growing things can bring you a sense of satisfaction and a feeling of oneness. As you plant seeds, fertilize, and pull weeds, you stimulate growth. Returning to the land, actually feeling the earth under your feet and in your hands, connects you to the natural order of things and brings joy to your heart.

- When you are constantly surrounded by the noise and demands of our modern world, you can feel cut off from spiritual nourishment. In contrast, gardening is an authentic act of creation; your decisions about what to plant, where to place which plants, and other touches are akin to the choices of artists and architects.

CARPE DIEM

Plan to create a small garden in the spring of the year. Plan for your garden to be bountiful and beautiful. Spend time nurturing each plant and every blooming flower. If you don't have the energy or desire to plant a garden, go visit one and enjoy the growth that will take place in the garden of your heart.

54.

BRACKET

- Our opinions and judgments are products of our egos. When we judge, we are laying claim to superior knowledge. We are saying that this thing is better than that thing, this person is better than that person.

- Judging squelches kindness. It impedes understanding. It blocks love.

- What if nothing is truly better than anything else—just different? And what if we simply loved instead of judging?

- Try bracketing your opinions about things and people now and then. Simply set them aside.

- When you find yourself thinking, "That's stupid" or "She's fat," change your thoughts to "That's not how I think about things, but I know that everyone is doing the best they can" or "She may be fat, but more important, I can see her flawless spirit."

CARPE DIEM

Today, when you find yourself judging, bracket those
thoughts and set them aside. See how you feel.

55.

SEEK YOUR TRUE SELF

- Deep down inside, you are a unique human being with passions and desires.

- What are those passions and desires? What brings you joy? Author and spiritual leader Sarah Ban Breathnach says that the authentic self is the soul made visible.

- Over the course of our lives, many of us conform to the expectations of society and end up losing touch with our passions and desires. We start living the life that is expected of us instead of the life that we were meant to live.

- When you are thinking and acting in congruence with your true self, you feel comfortable and joyful. When you are thinking and acting incongruently, you may feel a range of emotions, from boredom to anger to anxiety. How do you feel most of the time? Maybe now is the time to seek out your true self and begin to live your true life.

CARPE DIEM

In the coming week, every time you do something that makes you feel strong or that you lose yourself in, write it down. Every time you do something that makes you feel weak or anxious, write it down. At the end of the week, find patterns in your lists.

56.

WEAR A SYMBOL OF MOURNING

- In centuries past, mourners often made jewelry or wreaths out of locks of hair that belonged to the person who died. Black clothing was required for a period of one year. Mourners wore black armbands.

- These symbols of mourning accorded a special status to mourners, saying, in effect, "Someone I love has died. Please offer me your respect and your condolences."

- Today, we no longer identify mourners in these ways, creating the harmful illusion that "everything's back to normal"—even though it's not (and never will be).

- How do you let others know that you're still in mourning and still need their support? The best way is to tell them. Talk about the death and its continuing impact on your life. Let your friends and family know you still need their help.

CARPE DIEM

Make a symbol of mourning part of your everyday dress. Some people wear jewelry that belonged to the person who died. You might fill a locket with a photo and a lock of hair or wear a photo button on your jacket. Or sew a black armband and wear it proudly.

57.

REACH OUT AND TOUCH

- For many people, physical contact with another human being is healing. It has been recognized since ancient times as having transformative, healing powers.

- Have you hugged anyone lately? Held someone's hand? Put your arm around another human being?

- You probably know several people who enjoy hugging or physical touching. If you're comfortable with their touch, encourage it in the weeks and months to come.

- Hug someone you feel safe with. Kiss your children or a friend's baby. Walk arm in arm with a neighbor.

- You may want to listen to the song titled "I Know What Love Is," by Don White. I have found this song helps me reflect on the power of touch. Listen to this song then drop me a note or e-mail (DrWolfelt@ centerforloss.com) and let me know how it makes you think, and more important, feel.

CARPE DIEM

Try hugging your close friends and family members today,
even if you usually don't. You just might like it!

58.

EXPLORE TAI CHI

- Tai chi (pronounced "ty chee"), an ancient Chinese practice, is a gentle form of exercise that can both strengthen and nurture your spirit. It consists of thirteen postures that get your "good" energy flowing, thereby increasing your strength and creating resistance to "negative" energy.

- When you are physically, emotionally, and spiritually healthy, your life force, or chi, flows through you freely and you are fully alive. When you are stressed, and grief naturally brings stressful demands, challenges, and changes, your energy becomes blocked; you feel tired, depressed, out of balance, or even just a little bit "off." Or you may say, "I just don't feel like myself."

- Because your body is made up of integrated parts, when chi is blocked in one area, you may feel imbalance all over. The slow movements of tai chi calm you, inviting feelings of harmony into your body and feelings of being at peace with the world around you.

- Other martial arts are also considered spiritual practices. If tai chi isn't for you, try aikido or jujutsu.

CARPE DIEM

Locate a health club or exercise class in your community
that can introduce you to the practice of tai chi. Call
and make your first appointment right now.

59.

LISTEN

- We have five physical senses—sight, taste, hearing, touch, and smell—but most of us rely so heavily on our sense of sight that the other senses languish.

- As humans, we rely on sound for a great deal of our communication. But as you have no doubt learned, there is a big difference between hearing and listening. To connect on a spiritual level with others, you must listen.

- Music is ordered, constructed sound that can help you tap into your spiritual essence.

- Your brain remembers sound. If you try, you can conjure up the voice and the laughter of those you mourn. This exercise can help you feel closer to them.

CARPE DIEM

Step outside, sit or lie down someplace comfortable, close your eyes, and listen. What do you hear? Birds. Cars. The breeze riffling the leaves. Children playing. Imagine your spirit is a sound. What would it sound like today?

60.

LOSE TRACK OF TIME

- Most of us are so bound by our daily schedules that we forget that the notion of seconds, minutes, and hours is a man-made invention. Sure, the earth turns and the sun rises and sets, but if you listen to your body, it will set its own schedule.

- If you're constantly paying attention to the clock, you're probably not paying attention to your spirit and the here and now.

- Take your watch off for a day and don't peek at the clock on your cell phone, iPod, or PDA.

CARPE DIEM

Block out a day on your calendar when you
can be free to lose track of time.

61.

WALK BAREFOOT IN THE GRASS

- Few sensations bring me back to my childhood like walking barefoot in the lush green grass of early summer. Oh how refreshing to take off the trappings of adulthood—shoes and socks—and wiggle my toes in the cool, waxy blades.

- Grief deadens us. It naturally draws us within ourselves to a place we need to go before we can emerge again. But even while we are existing within this state of dormancy, we can and should emerge now and then to feel pleasure. Like other sensory experiences that are so rich we cannot help but be engaged by them, walking barefoot in the grass is a luscious reprieve.

- Lie in the grass. Put your face in it and breathe deeply. Roll down a grassy hill. And while you're at it, pick a dandelion and hold it under your chin to see if you like butter.

CARPE DIEM

Go to the biggest public park or field of grass in your community today, take off your shoes and socks, and walk and walk and walk barefoot in the green, green grass.

62.

WRITE A LETTER TO GOD

- Sometimes expressing our thoughts and feelings in letter-form helps us understand them better.

- Write a letter to God and express how you feel right now. Consider the following prompts:
    - Right now, my relationship with you is…
    - Right now, my journey through grief is…
    - My hopes for the future are…

- You might also find it helpful to write letters of gratitude to those people who were or continue to be supportive of you at this time, such as hospice staff, friends, family members, neighbors, doctors, nurses, funeral directors, etc.

CARPE DIEM

Write that letter to God and share it aloud with a trusted friend.

63.

RECONNECT WITH YOUR MAKER

- Grief often invites you to doubt your relationship with God. You may question the very existence of God or feel distant and alone. In the face of your grief, you may be angry at God. The good news is—God can take it!

- God doesn't leave us. We are the ones who may naturally retreat at times, particularly during times of loss and suffering. Yet God loves you no matter what you do or don't do. So if you are mad, have fears, concerns, or issues, take them to God.

- I know some people who, during times of grief, have been hurt by their faith communities and are apprehensive about God. Yet places of worship and the people who attend them are not God. Don't blame God for a bad experience you have had with people.

- Consider this: When you are in the midst of grief, you have a high need to feel understood and little capacity to be understanding. You are among the "walking wounded." If you look solely to other people for support, you will be discouraged and feel defeated. But if you turn to God, He will not forsake you, let you down, or hurt you. He may well be your refuge.

CARPE DIEM

Start the process of reconnecting with God, even if only in small steps. Begin by acknowledging something or someone you are grateful for.

64.

LOOK FOR THE SURPRISES
AND GIFTS IN YOUR DAY

- Stop reading this and look around you where you are right this
  moment. Look at the same things you see each day, but through a
  different set of eyes. What are you grateful for that is within your
  view? See it with awe. Look at the face of someone you love and
  rejoice that he is in your life.

- Whatever comes into your path today, consider it a gift. Take a
  moment to receive the gift and appreciate the giver. Embrace the
  warm feelings that come from being connected, from the link to
  gratefulness. Say "yes" and "thank you."

- Bill Keane said, "Yesterday's the past, tomorrow's the future, but
  today is a gift. That's why it's called the present."

CARPE DIEM

Create a "Surprise and Gift" Journal. Keep a running list of what
you are thankful for, the surprises that come to you each day,
and the gifts you receive. Be specific: I am thankful for the gift
of the gorgeous blue sky, the smile on my neighbor's face.

65.

USE A SINGING BOWL

- Singing bowls are used in Eastern spiritual traditions in meditation and prayer rituals. While they are made and used throughout Asia, the best-known types are from the Himalayas and are often called Tibetan singing bowls.

- Made of bronze and other metals, the bowls range in size from very small to very large. They "sing" when the user rubs a wooden mallet around the rim. Good quality bowls produce a harmonic tone.

- Place the bowl on a surface in front of you and strike the rim lightly with the mallet. Listen to the bell tone. Now try rubbing the mallet in a circular motion around the bowl's rim. Can you make it sing?

- Some singing bowl practitioners recommend that you lie down and place the bowl on your chest. This brings the sound close to your ears but also allows you to feel the vibrations throughout your body.

- The singing bowl's tone may help you relax and focus during meditation. It is also thought that the physical vibrations of the sound waves massage your body's cells and organs and release energy blockages.

CARPE DIEM

Place a photo of a person you mourn in the singing bowl.
As the bowl sings, imagine that the sound is carrying
your loving thoughts to the person who died. See if you
can hear back what the person might say to you.

66.

ACKNOWLEDGE YOUR CLOUD OF WITNESSES

- The Bible says that we are preceded and surrounded by a cloud of witnesses.

- Those whom we have loved and who have gone before us now serve as our witnesses. I like to think that they watch us with great fondness, forgiving our foibles and rejoicing in our kindnesses—and looking forward to the day when we will join them.

- Among our cloud of witnesses are untold others who also struggled with the death of someone loved, who also despaired in the "dark night of the soul." Some of the more learned and eloquent of these people wrote books about their experiences with despair and finding hope again. You might be helped by reading the writings of witnesses such as Henri Nouwen, C.S. Lewis and Catherine Marshall.

- Our cloud of witnesses also includes the great world and spiritual leaders who have shaped the course of history. Just think…what if Jesus and the Buddha and Lao Tzu are all hanging out together, watching us right now. What are they saying to each other?

CARPE DIEM

Pretend you could have dinner tonight with seven of the people in your cloud of witnesses. Who would you choose and why?

67.

BEAT THE DRUM

- Many cultures use the drum as part of their spiritual ceremonies.

- American Indians believe that the drum speaks to the drummer. The beating drum is akin to the beating heart and also represents the heartbeat of the earth. The animal skin that is stretched taut over the top of the drum brings the animal's soul to the dance as well.

- African tribes use drums to summon spirits to assist in positive change and healing.

- Pick up a drum and drum what you are feeling. Anger. Sadness. Fear. Release.

- You can play a drum as part of your meditation ritual. You can use any kind of drum. Tap it with your hands or use a drumstick. Beat a slow, steady rhythm. Time your breaths to the rhythm you have created. Breathe in...two...three...four. Breathe out...two...three... four.

- As your brain attends to the rhythm of the drum, your obsessive cares and worries fall away. This practice can be a very effective tool for relaxation and stress reduction.

CARPE DIEM

Stop by a music store today and learn about some different kinds of drums. See which one feels and sounds right to you.

68.

CREATE YOUR OWN WAILING WALL

- The Wailing Wall, also called the Western Wall, is the holiest place on earth for Jews. It is the remains of the great Jewish Temple in Jerusalem. Praying at the Wailing Wall signifies being in the presence of the Divine. Jews from all countries and tourists of other religious backgrounds come to pray at the wall, where it is said one immediately has the "ear of God." Those who cannot pray at the wall can send prayers or ask for the Kaddish to be said for departed loved ones. Prayers written on little pieces of paper, called *tzetzels*, are placed into the cracks of the wall.

- In the book (and movie) *The Secret Life of Bees*, author Sue Monk Kidd creates a character who builds her own wall of rocks in her back yard. When she is feeling full of pain, she writes her grief down and tucks it in between the rocks.

- You can create your own wailing wall—a place to mark your grief. Your wailing wall can literally be a rock wall in your garden in which you place notes about your grief. Or it could be a journal in which your write about your grief. Or it could be a jar in which you place little snippets of thoughts about your grief. Or a bulletin board. Or a box.

- Or maybe your wailing wall is a place where you can literally go to wail, to cry out in pain and anguish.

CARPE DIEM

Start a "wailing jar" today. Pick a suitable bowl or container and on a scrap of paper, write down a thought or a feeling about your grief journey. Fold up the paper and place it inside the jar. Add another thought and another whenever the mood strikes.

69.

PRAY WITH PRAYER BEADS

- Prayer beads are used in a number of faith traditions, including Islam, Catholicism, Buddhism, Hinduism and Baha'i.

- The person who is praying fingers the beads as he prays, and uses the pattern and number of the beads to keep track of which prayers and how many he has offered up.

- The repetitive motion of fingering the beads calms the mind and soothes the soul as the words of the prayer or the chant send your spiritual intentions into the beyond.

- If you do not strictly follow a specific religious doctrine, you may be interested in trying prayer beads as part of your spiritual practice. In his book *Simply Pray*, universalist minister Erik Walker Wikstrom suggests a modern prayer that uses a set of 28 beads. The practice includes centering and entering-in prayers, breath prayers, and prayers of Naming, Knowing, Listening and Loving. "Prayer beads are mobile alters," says Wikstrom.

CARPE DIEM

If you don't already have prayer beads, stop by a bead shop today and learn about buying or making a prayer strand.

70.

HOLD A NEWBORN

- Have you been lucky enough to hold a newborn baby lately? What a miracle is life!

- If you're a parent, you know that the birth of a baby is truly the most amazing moment you will ever experience.

- Many people believe that newborn babies are so recently spirit made flesh that they virtually vibrate with positive spiritual energy. They are humanity fresh from God.

- If you are mourning, you have recently experienced what we think of as the other end of life—the "sad" end. But what if indeed life is a circle and there is no end…only a continuum?

- Cuddle a baby and notice how it makes you feel. Find other ways to make this same feeling a part of your everyday life.

CARPE DIEM

The next time you're in the company of someone with a baby, ask permission to hold the little one for a few minutes. Silently bless the baby with your loving thoughts.

71.

GO TO THE WATER

- Many people find water to have a natural, healing quality during times of grief and loss. The gentle feeling of ocean waves washing up on the shoreline, the trickling of the mountain stream, the serenity of the quiet pond—all these aquatic sensations can offer comfort.

- Water invites you to return to the womb—to experience the sounds you heard even before being born. Water soothes the body and the soul. When you spend time near water, you connect back to its soothing, natural flow, allowing it to caress your wounded heart and return you back home feeling refreshed.

- Experiencing the tranquility that water brings into your life, you seek to match its serenity and in doing so, you become serene. Water reaches out to you in ways that calm your nerves and connect you with what is natural.

- Seek out opportunities to be near water and breathe in the beauty and wonder of nature. Close your eyes and repeat the following affirmation: "Water is pure and precious; water is healing; water is life."

CARPE DIEM

Schedule one hour of time to spend near water sometime within the next three days. Be quiet and listen as the water soothes your soul.

72.

BEAUTIFY YOUR ENVIRONMENT

- Many people believe that not only does the environment in which you live influence the way you think and feel, it is a reflection of the way you think and feel.

- How does your home environment mirror your inner life? Are they both chaotic, cluttered, ill-cared for? Read a bit about the principles of *feng shui*.

- First, de-clutter. Ask a friend or family member to help you. Complete one room at a time.

- Next, clean, or hire someone to clean. Either way, it's worth it.

- Now, freshen up the room with new paint, window coverings, pillows, etc. Hire a decorator for a one-hour consultation if you need help with this step.

- Finally, sit in your newly beautified room and relax. Notice how the room's energy affects your energy.

CARPE DIEM

Start small. De-clutter one drawer or one closet today. After,
see how the newly organized space makes you feel.

73.

STEP OUTSIDE YOUR COMFORT ZONE

- Not all spiritual practices are calm and Zen-like. Some things that make your heart race can also be good for your soul.

- Pushing beyond your boundaries and trying something you normally wouldn't is a good way to practice nonjudgment. After all, your boundaries are judgment lines. Everything within your boundaries is OK; everything outside them is not OK. But what if *everything* was really OK?

- If you're feeling stuck in your grief journey, this practice may be particularly helpful to you. There's no better way to get unstuck than to try moving in a different direction!

- Of course, I'm not advocating you do something illegal or harmful to yourself or others. I'm simply suggesting that you might be surprised at the new turns your life's path might take…if only you'd look right and left instead of just straight ahead.

CARPE DIEM

Today, say yes to something you normally wouldn't.

74.

TELL SOMEONE YOU LOVE THEM

- Your loss has you very aware of how love makes the world go round.

- Sometimes we love people so much, we forget to tell them "I love you." Or we (mistakenly) believe that they know they are loved, so we don't need to tell them.

- These three simple words have deep, spiritual meaning, yet we sometimes fail to see that until it's too late.

- My dad loved me, but it wasn't until just before his death that he whispered to me, "I love you." I miss you, Dad.

CARPE DIEM

Call someone you love right now and give her the
lasting gift of telling her you love her.

75.

PLAN A CEREMONY

- When words are inadequate, have ceremony.

- Ceremony assists in reality, recall, support, expression, transcendence.

- When personalized, the funeral ceremony can be a healing ritual. But ceremonies that take place later on can also be very meaningful. For example, a number of ceremonies have taken place at the site of the World Trade Center, and ceremonies will likely continue to be held there on the anniversaries of the tragedy. Ongoing ritual helps you continue to both remember and integrate the loss into your head, heart and soul.

- The ceremony might center on memories of the person who died, "meaning of life" thoughts and feelings, or affirmation of faith.

- In the Jewish body of faith there is a practice called Yizkor, the "remembering" prayer. Anyone in the synagogue who is not saying Yizkor is asked to leave until the prayer is completed. This ritual of having people leave is intended to protect the intimacy and sanctity of the sacred space for those who mourn.

CARPE DIEM

Hold a candle-lighting memory ceremony. Invite a small group of friends. Form a circle around a center candle, with each person holding their own small candle. Have each person light their memory candle and share a memory of the person who died. At the end, play a song or read a poem or prayer in memory of the person who died.

76.

GIVE THANKS TO GOD

- When you are faced with grief and suffering, it is naturally difficult to see some of the goodness that surrounds you. Yet, when you look for goodness in your life, you have more energy to do your "work of mourning." Yes, you are experiencing feelings of loss, but I ask you to consider thanking God for all that He has given you.

- The weight of grief gets very heavy. Let God carry some of that weight for you. Give that load to God and let Him keep it. Focus on that concept and you may discover that slowly, over time, you experience renewed energy, improved health, and some inner peace.

- It is okay to rest and ask for help. When you are in the midst of grief, you may not be able to see any blessings right now, but that is totally natural. Trust God that some blessings will come along the journey, even though you don't know what they look like just yet.

CARPE DIEM

Too often we take our blessings for granted. In fact,
make a list of everyone you are thankful for right now.
Then, thank God that these people are in your life!

77.

BEFRIEND YOUR MYSTICAL EXPERIENCES

- At some point in your grief, you may well have what is called a "mystical experience." One day, without warning, you may experience a sense of the presence of or a connection to the person who has died. You may hear his voice, feel her physical touch, see her appear to you, or experience a coincidence of some kind that seems impossible without otherworldly influence. Those experiences are usually not tinged in fear, but in comfort and joy. In fact, your mystical experience might be so awe-inspiring that you are forever changed by it.

- This direct encounter with the mystery surrounding love and loss is sacred and is an organic expression of the soul. When you experience these moments of mystery and intimate connection to those who have gone before you, befriend them as feelings of bliss.

- These breathtaking, sacred experiences of connection to your loved one are, in truth, benedictions of the Divine. Open yourself to these experiences and welcome them open-heartedly into your life. Don't think of them as "paranormal" events; think of them as sacred and divine experiences.

CARPE DIEM

Open yourself to the divine connection to those who have gone before you. When you have a "mystical experience," share it with a trusted friend who will be understanding and supportive.

78.

ENGAGE YOUR SPIRIT AT WORK

- Many people feel that their work lives are disconnected from their spiritual lives. They are one person when they are outside of work and they are a different, separate person when they are at work.

- That is not how the soul works. Your soul is your life force. It is present in all moments, in everything you do, say, think, believe.

- If you are separating yourself from your soul at work, you aren't living on purpose. You aren't honoring your true self and you are spending a huge percentage of your life in denial and darkness.

- You can engage your spirit at work in many ways. Always be kind to others. Speak your truth, and don't gossip. Take 5-minute meditation breaks. Go for a walk outdoors at lunchtime and immerse yourself in God's creation.

- If you find that your work deadens you, even after you have integrated such spiritual practices into your day, it's time to find a different job.

CARPE DIEM

Bring a spiritual totem to work and place it on your desk. It might be a photo or memento that connects you to the person who died. It might be a religious symbol. It might be a rock or other natural item. Place it somewhere you'll see it often, and when you are feeling stressed, turn your gaze to it and practice deep breathing.

79.

SIT IN THE SANCTUARY
OF STILLNESS

- Sitting in stillness with your grief will help you honor the deeper voices of quiet wisdom that come forth from within you. As Rainer Maria Rilke observed, "Everything is gestation and then bringing forth." In honoring your need to be still, you rest for the journey.

- Personal times of stillness are a spiritual necessity. A lack of stillness hastens confusion and disorientation and results in a waning of your spirit. Stillness restores your life force. Grief is only transformed when you honor the quiet forces of stillness.

- Yes, integration of grief is born out of stillness, not frantic movement forward. When you halt any instinct to attempt to "manage" your grief, other impulses such as grace, wisdom, love, and truth come forth. Any frantic attempts to quickly "move forward" or "let go" become counterproductive and deplete an already malnourished soul. It is through sitting with your stillness that your soul is ever so slowly restored.

CARPE DIEM

Take time right now to simply sit in stillness. As you do so, you will come to recognize that "the rhythm of stillness is the teacher of contentment and peace."

80.

VISIT THE GREAT OUTDOORS

- During times of grief and loss, many people find it restorative and energizing to spend time in nature. Returning to the natural world encourages you to discover what is essential both within you and the world around you.

- As a human being, you are a part of the natural world, and you are interdependent with it. As many naturalists would remind you, a close relationship with nature grounds your psyche and soul in the spiritual certainty of your roots. If you lose touch with nature's rhythms, you lose touch with your deepest self, with what some would call "the ground of your being."

- If you allow yourself to befriend nature, you will discover that its timeless beauty is renewing and healing. Observe how children respect and honor the spirit of nature and its beauty because they understand it instinctively. Flowers, birds, bugs, and butterflies often bring enthusiastic cries of recognition in children. You too can approach nature with the openness of a child. Take pleasure in the sounds, sights, and smells that fill your senses.

- Look up at the sky filled with beautiful clouds or twinkling stars. Stand barefoot in the cool grass. Play in the snow. Taste sweet strawberries from the field. Feel the wind and sun on your skin. It doesn't matter if you are in a garden or a park, in the mountains or beside the ocean. Mother Nature will soothe your soul and refresh your spirit.

CARPE DIEM

Today, reflect on your relationship with the natural world.
Go for a walk or hike and invite the Divine to come along.
Allow nature to sustain you and bring you peace.

81.

TAKE AN "ENCHANTED" BATH

- A warm bath invites you to rest your body and rejuvenate your spirit. As you prepare to create your bath, select an aromatic oil to calm and relax you. Add twenty-five drops to a full tub of water.

- Select music that relaxes you. Dim the lights and place a few candles around the tub.

- If you wish, add bubbles for fun, mineral salts for muscle relaxing, and a pillow to rest your head on.

- Prepare a nice herbal tea to drink while you are experiencing your nurturing bath. After your transforming soak, plan to wrap yourself up in a soft, cozy robe and curl up with a good book that feeds your soul. This magic bath experience can help re-light your "divine spark"—that which gives your life meaning and purpose!

CARPE DIEM

Go take your enchanted bath right now.

82.

WALK IN THE RAIN

- I live in Colorado, where it doesn't rain very often. But when it does, or when I am traveling to a location where it's rainy, I love to walk in the rain.

- As the raindrops fall, imagine they are washing away your despair. You are living in this moment, and in this moment, you are alive with the sensation of water running down your face. You are being baptized as a precious member of God's creation. You are here, now. The rain is here, now. The sound of your feet splashing through the puddles is here, now.

- Take an umbrella if you wish and enjoy the sound of rain pattering on the cloth. Or walk with no protection and allow the rain to soak into your very being.

CARPE DIEM

Go for a walk in the rain or snowfall. Try to clear your mind and pay attention instead to the sensation of cold and wetness on your cheeks and eyelashes. If it's snowing, make a snow angel or snowman!

83.

TRUST IN GOD

- It was C.S. Lewis who said, "I did not know that grief felt so much like fear." Sometimes, this natural fear can impact your capacity to trust God.

- Sometimes we wonder where God is when He isn't fixing something or instantly helping us feel better. We may feel abandoned by God and question his very existence.

- Yet, God is usually waiting for us to take action. When we do, He is right there beside us, "companioning" us through the grief journey.

- Sometimes it is difficult to remember that God has faith in us. As hard as it might be during times of loss and sadness, we must remind ourselves to trust in Him.

CARPE DIEM

Pray to God and tell Him you are going to lean on Him. When you feel tired and alone in your grief—and you will, lean on Him. Remind yourself that, as the saying goes: "If you see only one set of footprints in the sand, it is because God is carrying you."

84.

PRAY FOR OTHERS

- My hope is that other people are praying for you during this time of grief and loss in your life. I would also like to suggest that if you pray for others, your love and generosity will expand and flow.

- Beyond privately praying for other people, there are public ways in which you can pray for others. These include attending prayer services or joining a prayer group.

- A Buddhist prayer known as *metta* (loving kindness) is one approach you can do on your own. This involves praying over and over as a mantra, "May all beings be happy. May all beings be healthy. May all beings dwell in peace."

- As you begin your prayer time focusing on others, first quiet your mind and your body. Take some deep breaths. Close your eyes. Simply be still and rest in quiet solitude for a few minutes. Praying for your fellow human beings opens a doorway to your own new beginnings.

CARPE DIEM

Send prayers first to someone you love, then to someone you feel neutral about, and then to someone you feel challenged by.

85.

PAY ATTENTION TO SYNCHRONICITIES

- Stuff happens, the saying goes. (Well, you know the real saying, but this is a Godly book. ☺)

- The philosophy embedded in that aphorism is that things happen over which you have no control, and you need to resign yourself to the fact that life often sucks.

- Sometimes life does suck. Sometimes stuff happens. But often, if you are paying attention, if you are living on purpose, stuff happens that is nothing short of miraculous.

- At night you dream of a friend you haven't seen for years, and the next day she calls you, out of the blue. You hear a song on the car radio that perfectly captures what you're feeling that moment. Your furnace breaks down and you receive an unexpected check in the mail.

- Pay attention to coincidences. Believe that they may be telling you something—even guiding you. As the Dalai Lama said, "I am open to the guidance of synchronicity and do not let expectations hinder my path."

CARPE DIEM

The next time you experience what feels like a coincidence, write it down on your calendar. Contemplate what guidance it may be offering.

86.

CLIMB A MOUNTAIN

- For many people, climbing a mountain is an invigorating, soul-searching experience. There is something about mountains that invite you to discover the essentials within your spirit and the spirit of the world around you.

- Nature surrounds you as you hike upward, reflecting on a multitude of sights and sounds. Time in the mountains invites you to befriend the beauty of nature, allows you to experience tranquility, and restores your physical, emotional, and spiritual self.

- Being able to "peak" (make it to the top of) a gorgeous mountaintop affirms your physical, emotional, and spiritual strength. At the summit, the views are breathtaking, and you can celebrate and have gratitude for being alive. You have made it to the top of the world, surrounded by the power of Mother Nature. You are enveloped by the sights and the sounds, by the stillness and the solitude. You feel so close to God and your soul is calmed amid the grandeur of such spiritual beauty. You are one with the Divine. Feel your heart open and embrace the magic that surrounds you. Take a moment to close your eyes and remember the smiles of the person in your life who has died. Remember—this person is watching over you and cheering you on!

CARPE DIEM

Get your calendar out right now. Plan a date to make a trip to climb a mountain and allow yourself to be encapsulated in the beauty and power of Mother Nature.

87.

IMAGINE THE PERSON
WHO DIED IN HEAVEN

- Do you believe in an afterlife? Many mourners I have had the honor of companioning in their journeys are comforted by a belief or a hope that somehow, somewhere, their loved one lives on in health and happiness. For some, this belief is anchored in a religious faith. For others, it is simply a spiritual sense.

- If you do believe in an afterlife, you probably take comfort in having a continued spiritual relationship with the person who died. You probably have open, loving conversations with her. As Robert Benchley once noted, "Death ends a life, not a relationship." You can honor this need for continued communication while at the same time not allowing it to prevent you from interacting with and loving people who are still alive.

- You might find it healing to write a poem or a story or draw a picture of what the Heaven you imagine is like. Or you could create a collage. Cut out images from magazines and/or scrapbooking supplies that convey the look and feel of your Heaven, and assemble them together on a piece of poster board. Whenever your heart is heavy, spend a minute or two seeking solace in your Heavenly collage.

CARPE DIEM

Close your eyes right now and imagine what Heaven might be like. See the person you loved strong and smiling. Imagine her waving to you. And imagine your reunion with her when one day, you come to join her.

88.

GIVE THINGS AWAY

- You came into this world with nothing—literally, no things—and you will leave this world with nothing. But I'll bet that right now you have lots and lots of things!

- Is the sheer quantity of things you own burdening your spirit? Is it taking you more time, energy, and money to care for your things than it's worth?

- Maybe now is the time to give some stuff away. What do you have more of than you need?

- Try thinking of possessions as things that can come into and move out of your life easily. Easy come, easy go. They may enter your life for a specific reason at a specific time, but when you no longer need them, pass them on to someone who does.

- As you give away more and more of your possessions, you may feel a sense of lightening and clarity.

CARPE DIEM

Take one grocery store bag and walk with it through your house today. As you move from room to room, look for objects that you're not really using and don't truly care about. Place them in the bag until it's full, then drop off the bag at a donation box in your community.

89.

REASSESS YOUR PRIORITIES

- Death has a way of making us rethink our lives and the meaningfulness of the ways we spend them. It tends to awaken mourners to what is truly meaningful in life.

- What gives your life meaning? What doesn't? Take steps to spend more of your time on the former and less on the latter.

- Now may be the time to reconfigure your life. Choose a satisfying new career. Go back to school. Begin volunteering. Open yourself to potential new relationships. Help others in regular, ongoing ways. Move closer to your family.

- Many mourners have told me that they can no longer stand to be around people who seem shallow, egocentric, or mean-spirited. It's OK to let friendships wither with friends whom these adjectives now seem to describe. Instead, find ways to connect with people who share your new outlook on life—and death.

CARPE DIEM

Make a list with two columns: What's important to me.
What's not. Brainstorm for at least 15 minutes.

90.

LAUGH

- Humor is one of the most healing gifts of humanity. Laughter restores hope and assists us in surviving the pain of grief.

- Don't fall into the trap of thinking that laughing and having fun are somehow a betrayal of the person who died. Laughing doesn't mean you don't miss the person who died. Laughing doesn't mean you aren't in mourning.

- Sometimes it helps to think about what the person who died would want for you. Wouldn't she want you to laugh and continue to find joy in life, even in the midst of your sorrow?

- You can only embrace the pain of your loss a little at a time, in doses. In between the doses, it's perfectly normal, even necessary, to love and laugh.

- Remember the fun times you shared with the person who died. Remember his sense of humor. Remember his grin and the sound of his laughter.

- I've heard it said that laughter is a form of internal jogging. Not only is it enjoyable, it is good for you. Studies show that smiling, laughing, and feeling good enhance your immune system and make you healthier. If you act happy, you may even begin to feel some happiness in your life again.

CARPE DIEM

Close your eyes right now and try to remember the
smile and the laughter of the person who died.

91.

EMBRACE THE IMAGE OF THE EAGLE

- The image of the eagle is found across a broad range of spiritual beliefs and philosophies. Depending on the spiritual tradition, it symbolizes strength, courage, wisdom, spiritual protection and healing.

- The eagle's soaring flight has drawn comparisons to the holy spirit, intuition and grace.

- Some native cultures believe that the eagle carries our prayers to the Creator.

- There is a Native American blessing that says:

  May you have the strength
  Of eagles' wings,
  The faith and courage to
  Fly to new heights,
  And the wisdom
  Of the universe
  To carry you there.

CARPE DIEM

Listen to the song "On Eagles Wings" by Michael Joncas. Talk with a trusted friend about what this brings up for you.

92.

ESTABLISH A MEMORIAL FUND IN THE NAME OF THE PERSON WHO DIED

- Sometimes bereaved families ask that memorial contributions be made to specified charities in the name of the person who died. This practice allows friends and family members to show their support while helping the family feel that something good came of the death.

- You can establish a personalized and ongoing memorial to the person who died.

- What was deeply meaningful to the person who died? Did she support a certain nonprofit or participate in a certain recreational activity? Was she politically active? Is there an organization that tries to prevent the kind of death she suffered? What did she really and truly care about?

- Your local bank or funeral home may have ideas about how to go about setting up a memorial fund.

CARPE DIEM

Call another friend of the person who died and together brainstorm a list of ideas for a memorial. Suggest that both of you commit to making at least one additional phone call for information before the day is out.

93.

CREATE A PERSONAL SANCTUARY JUST FOR YOU

- When grief, loss, and the need to mourn enter your life, you need a dedicated safe space to call your own. You need a private territory where you can explore self-development and spiritual practices as well as read good books, meditate, journal, or simply contemplate the universe. When you understand that contemplate means "to create a space for the Divine to enter," perhaps you can acknowledge how important that space can be to your well-being.

- Places of worship (churches, temples, synagogues, mosques, monasteries, retreat centers) are usually sanctified to Divine work, meaning that in a formal way, with special prayers spoken, the building itself is "set apart" as a sacred space. Your home can also contain a sacred space where the sacred is found and cultivated.

- Find a cozy chair and consider installing a tabletop fountain. You may want to be able to play gentle music like sounds of the ocean, birds singing, or gentle drops of the rain forest. Or, maybe you want this space to be dedicated to silence. As Thomas Moore wisely noted, "Silence allows many sounds to reach awareness that otherwise would be unheard."

CARPE DIEM

Identify a space inside or outside of your home that can be your personal sanctuary. Make it a gentle, soothing space with well-chosen but minimal décor; clutter can feel chaotic. Lighting a candle each time you enter your space may help create a ritual of beginning. Now your sacred space becomes your spirit made manifest.

94.

NAME YOUR GRATITUDE & COUNT YOUR BLESSINGS

- When you are faced with loss, it can be difficult to feel a sense of gratitude in your life, yet gratitude prepares you for the blessings that are yet to come.

- Many blessings may have already companioned you since your grief journey began. Somehow, and with grace, you have survived. Looking back, you may recognize the many supportive gestures, big and small, you were offered along the way.

- When you fill your life with gratitude, you invoke a self-fulfilling prophecy. What you expect to happen *can* happen. For example, if you don't expect anyone to support you in your grief, they often don't. By contrast, if you anticipate support and nurturance, you will indeed find it.

- Think of all you have to be thankful for. This is not to deny you your overwhelming loss and the need to mourn. However, you are being self-compassionate when you consider the things that make your life worth living, too. Reflect on your possibilities for joy and love each day. Honor those possibilities and have gratitude for them. Be grateful for your physical health and your beautiful spirit. Be grateful for your family and friends and the concern of strangers. Above all, be grateful for this very moment. When you are grateful, you prepare the way for inner peace.

CARPE DIEM

Start keeping a gratitude journal. Each night before you go to bed, recount your blessings from the day. At first you may find this challenging, but as you continue this daily practice, it will get easier and more joyful.

95.

MANIFEST

- What have you always wanted to try, to do, to be, but haven't?

- I believe in callings. I believe that many people, perhaps all people, have feelings deep down inside about why they are here on Earth and what they are meant to do.

- I feel deeply that my calling is to help others learn to mourn well so they can go on to live well and love well. I know it's my calling because when I'm engaged in my teaching and writing, as I am right now, I feel joyful and in-the-moment. I feel energized and in touch with my center.

- Many people are afraid to engage with their calling because it seems frivolous or risky. Yet they continue to harbor a longing for it—a wistful longing that leaves them feeling frustrated, stuck, and sad.

- Now is the time to manifest your true self, to make it a reality. Keep in mind that you don't have to turn your current life upside down. You just have to take one small step today and another small step tomorrow and so on.

CARPE DIEM

Today, take one small step toward trying
something you've always wanted to try.

96.

BELIEVE IN THE POWER OF STORY

- Acknowledging a death is a painful, ongoing task that we accomplish in doses, over time. A vital part of healing in grief is often "telling the story" over and over again.

- The story of your relationship with the person who died might begin when you first met him and include many chapters along the way. You might find yourself wanting to talk about particular parts of the story more than others. Do you keep thinking about a certain moment or time period? If so, this means you should share this part of the story with others.

- What if you don't want to talk about it? It's OK to respect this feeling for weeks or months, but soon you'll need to start talking about it. Keeping your thoughts and feelings about the death inside you only makes them more powerful. Giving them voice allows you some control over them. Trust that you will "tell your story" when you are ready.

- Over time, your grief story will likely evolve from one dominated by the death itself to one dominated by loving memories of the person who died. This is a natural progression and a sign that you are healing.

- Find people who are willing to listen to you tell your story, over and over again if necessary, without judgment. These are often "fellow strugglers" who have had similar losses. But remember that not everyone will be able to be a compassionate listener. Your story may be a difficult one to hear. Seek out listeners who can be present to your pain.

CARPE DIEM

Today, discuss the story of the death with someone else who loved the person who died. Listen to and support each other.

97.

SEEK YOUR HIGHER SELF

- When you "live" in the realm of the Higher Self, you befriend divine qualities that are within you, such as caring, joy, strength, appreciation, and love. The Higher Self is the spiritual part of who you are. While the Higher Self recognizes that grief, loss, and sadness are part of the journey, it also realizes you can survive and slowly discover renewed meaning and purpose in your life.

- The Higher Self knows that all situations in life—happy and sad—can be used as times to learn and grow. It doesn't see the outside world as a threat; it sees it as a place to contribute and be hopeful about the future. Your Higher Self holds wisdom beyond your wildest dreams. This amazing wisdom can lead you into and through the wilderness of your grief. The Higher Self believes that out of the dark comes light, but that you must descend into grief before you transcend.

- If you listen to your Higher Self, this is what you might hear: "This loss brings me sadness and the need to grieve and mourn. Yet I will survive this painful part of my life and go on to enjoy the very best that life has to offer. Peace and laughter fill my heart."

CARPE DIEM

Remind yourself today to try to aspire to your Higher Self.

98.

LIVE ON PURPOSE.

- Do you believe that things happen for a reason? Do you think that you attract what you are thinking about?

- I'm not 100 percent sold on the popular concept of the power of attraction, but I have noticed that if I live with awareness and intention, I am able to live my best life.

- If you set your intention to mourn well and heal, and if you move forward each day embracing hope—even as you also embrace your pain, you are living on purpose. You are living with an awareness that your intentional thoughts create, in part, your destiny.

- You are a miracle. Your life is a miracle. Live it with the awe and wonder it deserves.

CARPE DIEM

Today, set your intention for the coming year. With what attitude do you intend to live each day? How do you intend to mourn so that you can learn to love and live well again?

99.

BELIEVE IN YOUR CAPACITY TO HEAL

- All the veteran grievers I have ever had the privilege of meeting and learning from would want me to tell you this: You will survive.

- If your loss was recent, you may think you cannot get through this. You can and you will. It may be excruciatingly difficult, yes, but over time and with the love and support of others, your grief will soften and you will find ways to be happy again. There will come a day when the death is not the first thing you think of when you wake up in the morning.

- Many mourners also struggle with feeling they don't *want* to survive. Again, those who have gone before you want you to know that while this feeling is normal, it will pass. One day in the not-too-distant future you will feel that life is worth living again. For now, think of how important you are to your children, your partner, your parents and siblings, your friends.

- As you actively mourn, you may also choose not simply to survive, but to truly live. The remainder of your life can be full and rich and satisfying if you choose life over mere existence.

CARPE DIEM

If you're feeling you won't make it through the next few weeks or months, talk to someone about your feelings of panic and despair. The simple act of expressing these feelings may render them a little less powerful. Remember—grief waits on welcome, not on time.

100.

DANCE THROUGH GRIEF INTO LIFE

- Dance has been described as a metaphor for life. In the midst of grief, dance can be a lovely way to transform your grief (your internal response) into mourning (the shared outward response). Dance invites you to merge with the music and the movement even as it takes you outside of yourself.

- Constanze referred to dancing as dreaming with your feet. Sweetpea Tyler claimed it faces you toward heaven, whichever direction you turn. Havelock Ellis described it as life itself. Martha Graham called it the hidden language of the soul.

- Dance is more than an aerobic physical activity. It is a complete mind, body, and spirit workout, and it is fun! (God knows you need some fun in the wilderness of grief.) Many forms of dance are forms of moving meditation. The blend of physical, emotional, and spiritual concentration invite both surrender and renewal, while at the same time transporting you into a spiritual realm of wholeness and connection to the world outside of yourself. Yes, there is magic in dance.

- Dance can transform you in ways that re-awaken your divine spark— "that which gives life meaning and purpose." Movement allows your body to heal, your mind to open, and your spirit to sing. Dance also engages you in community because you enter into a partnership that is greater than the sum of its parts. You discover that you are in constant, ever-flowing exchange with yourself, each other, and the Divine.

CARPE DIEM

Take some dance lessons. Salsa, ballroom, ballet, tap, clogging, jazz, belly dancing? Pick one and call today to get started.

A FINAL WORD

Hope is the thing with feathers

That perches in the soul

And sings the tune without the words

And never stops at all.

—Emily Dickinson

You have no doubt heard the wisdom-filled words, "Blessed are those who mourn, for they shall be comforted." To this I might add, "Blessed are those who nurture themselves spiritually, for they shall go on to discover continued meaning in life, living, and loving.

Spiritual self-care fortifies you for the ongoing ebbs and flows of your grief journey, a journey which leaves you profoundly affected and deeply changed. In part, to nurture yourself spiritually is to pay attention to your needs. When we recognize that spiritual self-care during times of loss and grief invites us to be alert and aware of the world around us, we can mourn in ways that help us heal.

I also believe that spiritual self-care is about taking time to enjoy the moment, to find hidden treasures everywhere—a child's smile, a beautiful sunrise, a flower in bloom, a friend's gentle touch. Spirituality invites us to be open to the mystery as we live fully in the present, remembering our past, and embracing our future.

Spirituality invites us to simplify our lives so we can be open to giving and receiving love. We need a sense of belonging, a sense of meaning, a sense of purpose. Realizing that we belong helps us feel safe and secure.

Spirituality invites us to remember that we have only now to let people know that we love them. There is magic and miracles in loving and being loved. Yes, "Love…bears all things, believes all things, hopes all things, endures all things. Love never ends."

One final "carpe diem" for you: Call someone right now and let them know how their gentle and loving spirit sustains you.

Bless you. I hope we meet one day.

THE MOURNER'S CODE

Ten Self-Compassionate Principles

Though you should reach out to others as you journey through grief, you should not feel obligated to accept the unhelpful responses you may receive from some people. You are the one who is grieving, and as such, you have certain "rights" no one should try to take away from you.

The following list is intended both to empower you to heal and to decide how others can and cannot help. This is not to discourage you from reaching out to others for help, but rather to assist you in distinguishing useful responses from hurtful ones.

1. **You have the right to experience your own unique grief.** No one else will grieve in exactly the same way you do. So, when you turn to others for help, don't allow them to tell you what you should or should not be feeling.

2. **You have the right to talk about your grief.** Talking about your grief will help you heal. Seek out others who will allow you to talk as much as you want, as often as you want, about your grief. If at times you don't feel like talking, you also have the right to be silent.

3. **You have the right to feel a multitude of emotions.** Confusion, numbness, disorientation, fear, guilt and relief are just a few of the emotions you might feel as part of your grief journey. Others may try to tell you that feeling angry, for example, is wrong. Don't take these judgmental responses to heart. Instead, find listeners who will accept your feelings without condition.

4. **You have the right to be tolerant of your physical and emotional limits.** Your feelings of loss and sadness will probably leave you feeling fatigued. Respect what your body and mind are telling you. Get daily rest. Eat balanced meals.

And don't allow others to push you into doing things you don't feel ready to do.

5. **You have the right to experience "griefbursts."** Sometimes, out of nowhere, a powerful surge of grief may overcome you. This can be frightening, but it is normal and natural. Find someone who understands and will let you talk it out.

6. **You have the right to make use of ritual.** The funeral ritual does more than acknowledge the death of someone loved. It helps provide you with the support of caring people. More importantly, the funeral is a way for you to mourn. If others tell you the funeral or other healing rituals such as these are silly or unnecessary, don't listen.

7. **You have the right to embrace your spirituality.** If faith is a part of your life, express it in ways that seem appropriate to you. Allow yourself to be around people who understand and support your religious beliefs. If you feel angry at God, find someone to talk with who won't be critical of your feelings of hurt and abandonment.

8. **You have the right to search for meaning.** You may find yourself asking, "Why did he or she die? Why this way? Why now?" Some of your questions may have answers, but some may not. And watch out for the clichéd responses some people may give you. Comments like, "It was God's will" or "Think of what you have to be thankful for" are not helpful and you do not have to accept them.

9. **You have the right to treasure your memories.** Memories are one of the best legacies that exist after the death of someone loved. You will always remember. Instead of ignoring your memories, find others with whom you can share them.

10. **You have the right to move toward your grief and heal.** Reconciling your grief will not happen quickly. Remember, grief is a process, not an event. Be patient and tolerant with yourself and avoid people who are impatient and intolerant with you. Neither you nor those around you must forget that the death of someone loved changes your life forever.

WANTED:
YOUR SPIRITUAL SELF-CARE IDEAS

Please help me write the next edition of this book. I will plan to update and rewrite this book every few years. For this reason I would really like to hear from you. Please write and let me know about your experience with this book.

If an Idea is particularly helpful to you, let me know. Better yet, send me an Idea you have that you think other fellow mourners might find helpful. When you write to me, you are "helping me help others" and inspiring me to be a more effective grief companion, author, and educator.

Thank you for your help. Please write to me at:

Alan D. Wolfelt
Center for Loss and Life Transition
3735 Broken Bow Road
Fort Collins, CO 80526
Or email me at DrWolfelt@centerforloss.com or go to our website, www.centerforloss.com.

My idea:

_____

_____

_____

_____

My name and mailing address:

_____

_____

_____

ALSO BY ALAN WOLFELT

Understanding Your Grief
Ten Essential Touchstones for Finding Hope and Healing Your Heart

One of North America's leading grief educators, Dr. Alan Wolfelt has written many books about healing in grief. This book is his most comprehensive, covering the essential lessons that mourners have taught him in his three decades of working with the bereaved.

In compassionate, down-to-earth language, *Understanding Your Grief* describes ten touchstones—or trail markers—that are essential physical, emotional, cognitive, social, and spiritual signs for mourners to look for on their journey through grief.

The Ten Essential Touchstones:

1. Open to the presence of your loss.
2. Dispel misconceptions about grief.
3. Embrace the uniqueness of your grief.
4. Explore what you might experience.
5. Recognize you are not crazy.
6. Understand the six needs of mourning.
7. Nurture yourself.
8. Reach out for help.
9. Seek reconciliation, not resolution.
10. Appreciate your transformation.

Think of your grief as a wilderness—a vast, inhospitable forest. You must journey through this wilderness. To find your way out, you must become acquainted with its terrain and learn to follow the sometimes hard-to-find trail that leads to healing. In the wilderness of your grief, the touchstones are your trail markers. They are the signs that let you know you are on the right path. When you learn to identify and rely on the touchstones, you will find your way to hope and healing.

ISBN 978-1-879651-35-7 • 176 pages • softcover • $14.95

Companion
PRESS

All Dr. Wolfelt's publications can be ordered by mail from:
Companion Press
3735 Broken Bow Road
Fort Collins, CO 80526
(970) 226-6050
www.centerforloss.com

ALSO BY ALAN WOLFELT

The Understanding Your Grief Journal

Exploring the Ten Essential Touchstones

Writing can be a very effective form of mourning, or expressing your grief outside yourself. And it is through mourning that you heal in grief.

The Understanding Your Grief Journal is a companion workbook to Dr. Wolfelt's *Understanding Your Grief.* Designed to help mourners explore the many facets of their unique grief through journaling, this compassionate book interfaces with the ten essential touchstones. Throughout, journalers are asked specific questions about their own unique grief journeys as they relate to the touchstones and are provided with writing space for the many questions asked.

Purchased as a set together with *Understanding Your Grief,* this journal is a wonderful mourning tool and safe place for those in grief. It also makes an ideal grief support group workbook.

ISBN 978-1-879651-39-5 • 150 pages • softcover • $14.95

Companion

All Dr. Wolfelt's publications can be ordered by mail from:
Companion Press
3735 Broken Bow Road
Fort Collins, CO 80526
(970) 226-6050
www.centerforloss.com

ALSO BY ALAN WOLFELT

The Wilderness of Grief

Finding Your Way

A beautiful, hardcover gift book version of *Understanding Your Grief*

Understanding Your Grief provides a comprehensive exploration of grief and the ten essential touchstones for finding hope and healing your heart. *The Wilderness of Grief* is an excerpted version of *Understanding Your Grief*, making it approachable and appropriate for all mourners.

This concise book makes an excellent gift for anyone in mourning. On the book's inside front cover is room for writing an inscription to your grieving friend.

While some readers will appreciate the more in-depth *Understanding Your Grief*, others may feel overwhelmed by the amount of information it contains. For these readers we recommend *The Wilderness of Grief*. (Fans of *Understanding Your Grief* will also want a copy of *The Wilderness of Grief* to turn to in spare moments.)

The Wilderness of Grief is an ideal book for the bedside or coffee table. Pick it up before bed and read just a few pages. You'll be carried off to sleep by its gentle, affirming messages of hope and healing.

ISBN 978-1-879651-52-4 • 128 pages • hardcover • $15.95

Companion

All Dr. Wolfelt's publications can be ordered by mail from:
Companion Press
3735 Broken Bow Road
Fort Collins, CO 80526
(970) 226-6050
www.centerforloss.com

ALSO BY ALAN WOLFELT

Living in the Shadow of the Ghosts of Grief

Step into the Light

Reconcile old losses and open the door to infinite joy and love

"*Accumulated, unreconciled loss affects every aspect of our lives.*
Living in the Shadow *is a beautifully written compass with the needle ever-pointing in the direction of hope.*"
— Greg Yoder, grief counselor

"*So often we try to dance around our grief. This book offers the reader a safe place to do the healing work of "catch-up" mourning, opening the door to a life of freedom, authenticity and purpose.*"
— Kim Farris-Luke, bereavement coordinator

Are you depressed? Anxious? Angry? Do you have trouble with trust and intimacy? Do you feel a lack of meaning and purpose in your life? You may well be living in the shadow of the ghosts of grief.

When you suffer a loss of any kind—whether through abuse, divorce, job loss, the death of someone loved or other transitions, you naturally grieve inside. To heal your grief, you must express it. That is, you must mourn your grief. If you don't, you will carry your grief into your future, and it will undermine your happiness for the rest of your life.

This compassionate guide will help you learn to identify and mourn your carried grief so you can go on to live the joyful, whole life you deserve.

ISBN 978-1-879651-51-7 • 160 pages • softcover • $13.95

Companion
P R E S S

All Dr. Wolfelt's publications can be ordered by mail from:
Companion Press
3735 Broken Bow Road
Fort Collins, CO 80526
(970) 226-6050
www.centerforloss.com

ALSO BY ALAN WOLFELT

The Journey Through Grief
Reflections On Healing
Second Edition

This popular hardcover book makes a wonderful gift for those who grieve, helping them gently engage in the work of mourning. Comforting and nurturing, *The Journey Through Grief* doses mourners with the six needs of mourning, helping them soothe themselves at the same time it helps them heal.

Back by popular demand, we are now offering *The Journey Through Grief* again in hardcover. The hardcover version of this beautiful book makes a wonderful, healing gift for the newly bereaved.

This revised, second edition of *The Journey Through Grief* takes Dr. Wolfelt's popular book of reflections and adds space for guided journaling, asking readers thoughtful questions about their unique mourning needs and providing room to write responses.

The Journey Through Grief is organized around the six needs that all mourners must yield to—indeed embrace—if they are to go on to find continued meaning in life and living. Following a short explanation of each mourning need is a series of brief, spiritual passages that, when read slowly and reflectively, help mourners work through their unique thoughts and feelings. *The Journey Through Grief* is being used by many faith communities as part of their grief support programs.

ISBN 978-1-879651-11-1 • hardcover • 176 pages • $21.95

Companion

All Dr. Wolfelt's publications can be ordered by mail from:
Companion Press
3735 Broken Bow Road
Fort Collins, CO 80526
(970) 226-6050
www.centerforloss.com